Drawn to the Light

Germaine Chevarie

Order this book online at www.trafford.com
or email orders@trafford.com

Most Trafford titles are also available at major online book retailers.

Printed in Victoria, BC, Canada.

ISBN: 978-1-4269-2123-0 (sc)

ISBN: 978-1-4269-2124-7 (dj)

Library of Congress Control Number: 2009941110

*Our mission is to efficiently provide the world's finest, most comprehensive book publishing
service, enabling every author to experience success. To find out how to publish your book, your
way, and have it available worldwide, visit us online at www.trafford.com*

Trafford rev. 12/21/2009

 www.trafford.com

North America & international
toll-free: 1 888 232 4444 (USA & Canada)
phone: 250 383 6864 ♦ fax: 812 355 4082

Note From The Author

This book has been written in the hope that the younger generation, especially our grandchildren, will never lose interest in reading. Literacy is most important in the development of all human being's intellectual capacity. I also want to prove that learning a second language or even a third language is attainable. Even though I have never attended an English school, I have learned the English language by reading books upon books. The legacy I want to leave our grandchildren is the knowledge which can only be acquired by reading. With today's technology, it has become too easy to look at a screen and press buttons instead of opening a book and getting interested enough in the story to keep reading to the end. There will always be good books and not so good books, but the benefits of reading any book will be the same.

In the hope of holding my grandchildren's interest, I have used their names throughout this book. It is a fictional story and not meant to be taken literally. I remember listening to my own grandfather telling us all kinds of interesting and wonderful stories which kept us occupied for hours. Even though my grandfather couldn't read or write, he was very articulate and had a vivid imagination, but not everyone is like that. Therefore, I like to think of this book as a story- telling book. I also like to believe that I've inherited some of my grandfathers' gifts. One of them was a story-teller and the other, a tealeaf reader.

I have met our young magician Rémi Boudreau personally when I attended one of his magic shows in Rogersville, New Brunswick. Needless to say how impressed I was with his magic. It was superb! He even got me involved in one of his magic tricks. It was so exciting!

Always remember that in your own mind, you can be anyone you'd like to be, you can dream of anything you'd like to do or imagine anyplace you'd like to go. No one can stop you from thinking. That is one area in your life that is yours alone, to be shared only if you so wish. But remember, it is always more fun to share your gifts and that includes sharing your thoughts. If Albert Einstein or Alexander Graham Bell hadn't shared their thoughts with other people, think of how much we would have missed? Who is to say 'you' are not the next inventor of something big?

Ten percent of my net proceeds from the sales of this book will be donated to a local Literacy Program. In this day and age, no one should go through life being unable to read or write.

Whether you are young or old, I hope you enjoy reading my book.

God bless!

DEDICATION

This book is dedicated with love to my whole family. First, to my loving husband of 44 years Gerard, to our five great children and our eight beautiful grandchildren.

Also, to my seven sisters and my six brothers who are all so dear to me.

A special rememberance to our Dad who passed away suddenly on February 7/08 and most recently, to the best Mother in the whole world whom God also welcomed home on July 14/09. Their spirits will always be alive through their 14 children, 39 grandchildren and 41 great-grandchildren. "Even though you die, you shall live"

Prologue

Joel Harmon and Francis (Frisco) O'Brien were a couple of ordinary teenagers who had become best friends in elementary school. The events that were to unfold shortly before graduation taught them that anything is possible when one sets his mind to it! But they also learned to rely on a higher power when things seemed impossible and that God's presence is always there, no matter what.

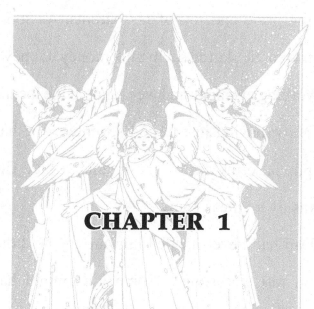

CHAPTER 1

Francis O'Brien, better known to his friends and family members as Frisco, was parked by the ocean water's edge, waiting for his friend Joel Harmon to join him. Both were in their last year of High School with graduation only six weeks away. Like most teenagers, Frisco and Joel's biggest concern was the upcoming prom dance and the difficult decision of who they were going to ask to be their date. That was one of the reasons they had agreed to meet by the wharf on that particular late afternoon, in early Summer .

Frisco was a well-adjusted young man who didn't drink to excess and kept away from drugs. Being an only child, he was the pride and joy of his parents. As soon as he turned sixteen, he started saving his money, money that he earned working evenings and weekends at the local service station. Now, having just turned seventeen, he had been able to purchase the car of his dreams, a blue Corvette, which was by no means new.

His Dad had never handed him money he didn't earn except on rare occasions. Some kids might have felt deprived, but not Frisco. He knew that he had something a lot of his classmates didn't have, the unconditional love of both his Mom and his Dad.

Joel, with his auburn hair, was very handsome and also a well adjusted young man who unlike Frisco, had two younger siblings, Kelsey who was eighteen months his junior and a little brother Andy, five years younger than Kelsey. Joel's family had moved next door to the O'Briens twelve years earlier. His parents, Trent and Edith Harmon, had decided to leave their home in Newfoundland to move to New Brunswick after visiting a distant relative on Grand Manan Island. They had been drawn to Black's Harbour, a small community in South Western New Brunswick where the Sardine Industry and the ocean beckoned them as they boarded the ferry taking them to the island of Grand Manan, an island very popular in New Brunswick during the tourist season. They had heard great things about Black's Harbour, especially because work was plentiful and the wages were fair.

It was at a time when work was very scarce in their small community of Evandale in Newfoundland, because the cod industry was failing and Trent Harmon was worried that his growing family would not be able to survive the low economic trend that was taking place. They could hardly make ends meet as it was and if it hadn't been for their ailing aunt on Grand Manan Island, they certainly wouldn't have spent the little money they had saved on a trip. Trent and Edith wanted to do all they could for their three children so upon their return home, they made arrangements to move to Black's Harbour. Five weeks later, they had sold their house in Evandale and came all the way back to New Brunswick with only what would fit on the back of their pick-up truck. A few days were all it took to find and settle in a good size home right on Main Street. They left their hotel room feeling confident that they had done the right thing.

The children were registered in their new school and seemed to take an instant liking to the community and its inhabitants. In a way, it felt as if they were still in their native land, only here work was plentiful especially from May to December. Their closest neighbors, Cain and Gabrielle O'Brien, (Frisco's parents) welcomed them with hot casseroles and home-made pies. Their son and the Harmon's kids had become instant friends.

As the two families grew up together, the parents also became friends. While the children played together practically every day, Edith and Gabrielle shared recipes and stories of the past. Trent and Cain went fishing just about every weekend, sometimes bringing all four kids.

As the two older boys became teenagers, Kelsey could often be seen tagging along with them and Frisco teasing her unmercifully. Countess times he brought her to tears by calling her "curly" because of her dark curly hair. Then all at once he stopped teasing her and Kelsey could have sworn he went out of his way to avoid even talking to her.

Kelsey had nurtured a crush on her brother's friend Frisco for the past couple of years, but would have died of embarrassment if anyone, much less Frisco, had found out about it. She missed the 'old' days when his teasing had brought her to tears. Being teased was better than being ignored! To Kelsey's chagrin, Frisco started dating a girl she knew and jealousy was eating away at her young heart. Luckily their dating didn't last very long!

Lately, it seemed every time she addressed him, Frisco's eyes wandered away from her face which made her feel very uncomfortable. What could she possibly have done to make him act this way? Her question remained unanswered for there was no one she felt comfortable enough to confide in.

In desperation, she thought of talking to her little brother Andy about it but then decided against it. Andy would probably go right to Frisco and tell him what his sister had said and that was the last thing she wanted to happen. Her Mother was out of the question because she never seemed to understand the opposite sex. How many times had she heard her Mom say; "I don't understand how men think, it's a complete mystery to me." Now Kelsey understood her mother's words or so she thought, because for the life of her, she couldn't understand why Frisco was treating her the way he did. The only one left to confide in was her Dad. He was honest and she trusted that he would at least try to enlighten her on this very delicate and personal subject. Kelsey didn't even consider talking to Joel about it. He would probably just make fun of her. Yes, her only option was her father. But her dad seemed to be at a loss for words when she finally got enough courage to bring it up. His only advice was that 'boys did that sometimes, ignored the girls that is. It didn't mean that they didn't like them.' Therefore Kelsey kept on being miserable.

This went on until the day she turned fifteen. Frisco and his family had been invited for cake and ice-cream as they had on many other occasions. For reasons unknown to her, Frisco began to acknowledge that she was indeed alive! It made Kelsey very happy but she still kept her secret. Nobody knew how she really felt about Frisco.

Frisco would have picked up Joel at his house as usual, in the famous Corvette, but Joel had a dental appointment that day and his Mom had taken him into town. This was why Frisco stood by himself throwing rocks into the Bay of Fundy near the Ferry Terminal, watching the ripples on the water after each throw. Joel had promised to come join him as soon as he and his Mom were back from the dentist's office.

"Why aren't they back?" Frisco wondered aloud. It was way past suppertime and there was still no sign of them. Frisco was getting restless and worried, more so when he saw his Dad's car approaching the Ferry Terminal. As the car drew closer, he saw that Kelsey was with his Dad. .

"What in the world is Kelsey doing here with Dad?" he wondered. As soon as the car came to a stop, Kelsey jumped out and ran out toward him. This time, Frisco didn't ignore her.

"What is it Kelsey? Where is Joel and why are you here with Dad"? Kelsey looked at him and barely whispered, "Oh Frisco, there's been an accident".

"An accident, what do you mean? Who had an accident?" Frisco was beginning to panic.

Her voice trembling, Kelsey replied, "Did you know Mom was taking Joel to the dentist today?"

"Yes, that's why I'm here by myself. He was going to meet me here afterward".

"He's not coming Frisco." Kelsey said between sobs.

"He's in the hospital and so is Mom." By this time, Cain O'Brien was standing beside his son.

"Leave your car here Frisco and come with Kelsey and I to the Fundy Health Center. Thank goodness you're here. Kelsey said she knew exactly where to find you and she was right."

"Let's go!" Frisco said, already on his way to the car.

When they arrived at the Health Center, they were met in the lobby by Joel's Dad. The Harmon's, Trent and Edith were well known in the community. Trent was an engineer at the Plant and Edith was one of the two hairdressers in the area. Therefore, the nursing staff at the Health Center was treating them as members of their own families. It was with great relief that they heard the good news that both Joel and Edith were in stable condition, and only as a precaution were they being transferred to the Regional Hospital in Saint John for overnight observation. Trent informed Cain that their car had been completely demolished. The other car's lone occupant had apparently fallen asleep at the wheel and unlike Joel and his Mom, had not survived the crash. The police had told Trent Harmon how fortunate he was that both his wife and son had come out of this accident with only minor injuries, maybe a concussion at the most. The attending doctor had also assured him that as far as he could see, there were no broken bones. Both Joel and Edith would be very sore for the next few days but he didn't foresee any long-term complications.

Frisco and Kelsey wanted to see for themselves if Joel and Edith were O.K. and the doctor agreed to let them go in. Dr. Reed had known these teenagers since they were knee high. He gave them ten minutes to visit with them since his two patients would be leaving for the Regional Hospital soon. Without giving it a second thought, Frisco took Kelsey's hand as they started walking toward the Emergency Room. The two fathers looked at each other as if to say, 'Did you see that? What is going on here?' Their question remained unanswered as Trent said to his long-time friend and neighbor; "Cain, if you want to go home, it's O.K., Frisco can come home with Kelsey and I".

"Yes," replied Cain, "I think I will go home if you're sure you don't need me here."

"I suppose Gabrielle is anxious to hear what happened. Go ahead; everything seems to be under control. I'm just so thankful they weren't seriously hurt. I'll talk to you later."

As soon as the emergency room door closed behind them, Kelsey reluctantly let go of Frisco's hand and ran to her mother's bedside.

"How do you feel Mom, do you hurt anywhere"?

"No honey, I'm fine. Don't worry about me dear, Dr. Reed said he would give me something to help me have a good night's sleep so I can go home, hopefully tomorrow."

While Kelsey was talking with her mom, Frisco went to see Joel who was in the next bed behind a curtain divider.

Pushing the curtain aside, he took one step toward Joel's bed and came to a halt. Something was wrong! Joel's eyes were fluttering and he was beginning to shake all over. Reacting quickly, he rang for a nurse who immediately came in. One look at Joel and she knew he was going into convulsions.

"Get Dr. Reed right away!" the nurse told Frisco. A petrified Frisco ran out to get Dr. Reed who happened to be walking by. With the ensuing commotion behind the curtained bed, Kelsey and her mom knew something was terribly wrong with Joel. The only thing that kept Kelsey from freaking out was her concern for her mother.

In what seemed like forever, but only minutes in reality, the ambulance attendants and a nurse had Joel on a stretcher and in an ambulance on their way to the Saint John Regional Hospital with lights flashing. At a slower pace, Trent followed in the other ambulance that was taking Edith to the same Hospital. Frisco and Kelsey went in Trent's car so they would have a vehicle to return home.

It was a long and tense 40 minute drive. They drove in silence most of the way, afraid of voicing their concern for Joel. A few times, Frisco reassured Kelsey that Joel would be fine. Trent was also trying to reassure Edith that Joel would be fine but deep inside he was really worried.

When they arrived at the Emergency Department of the Saint John Regional Hospital, they were met by a nurse who led them to a Doctor. Dr. Halloway assured them that Joel was out of danger and in very good hands. Edith was wheeled into a room while the other three were asked to go to the waiting room. A nurse told them the doctor would be in later to talk with them and showed them the way to the waiting room and to the coffee and pop machine.

About an hour later, Dr. Halloway, the on-call physician in the ER that evening, followed by a surgeon whose mask was still dangling from his neck, walked into the room and asked to speak to Joel Harmon's dad. At this point, everyone was a bundle of nerves and the three jumped up at the same time.

After introducing himself as well as Dr. Kennedy, a neurosurgeon, Dr. Halloway gave them an update of Joel's condition and prognosis.

"Your son is a fighter Mr. Harmon. But I have to tell you that he scared us for a few minutes. We lost his heartbeat when all of a sudden; he opened his eyes and looked around the room, telling us that everything was beautiful. He then closed his eyes again and fell into a very deep sleep. His vital signs have since returned to normal. Amazing boy"! Shaking his head, he continued: "I'll let Dr. Kennedy explain to you what happened to cause his convulsions. He's the expert".

"As Dr. Halloway mentioned, your son is indeed a lucky boy! After reading the P.E.T. scan, we discovered a blood clot very close to his brain. I was ready to do surgery when fortunately, it dissolved before it reached the brain. That boy can count his many blessings! Why don't you all go home for a couple of hours rest? Dr. Halloway will recheck him before he leaves tonight. Don't worry, I know a fighter when I see one, and that boy will be around for a long time. Although his condition has stabilized, I would rather he not be disturbed the rest of the night. He will have to stay in for a few days so you can visit with him tomorrow".

Joel's dad nodded his head for he was too moved to say anything. Dr. Kennedy left the room bidding everyone goodnight.

"You're sure he'll be O.K. Doctor Halloway?" Kelsey sniffled. "We should go tell Mom, she must be worried."

"I've already taken care of that" replied the good doctor, "but go ahead, all of you. Stay only long enough to say good-night because she also needs to rest."

"Sure Doctor, we understand" Frisco replied.

Frisco, Kelsey and her Dad left the waiting room to go see how Edith was feeling. As they were about to get on the elevator, they spotted Frisco's parents, Cain and Gabrielle, in the hospital's lobby. Trent waved to get their attention and the O'Brien's quickly joined them. Gabrielle had been worried sick about Edith and Joel, so Cain had

driven back to Saint John so she'd be closer if Edith should

need her. In any case, they both felt the need to be there to

offer support to their best friends.

On the way to Edith's room, Frisco filled his parents in

on the good news about Joel. Edith seemed very pleased

to see Gabrielle. After a few minutes, Edith mentioned

their youngest son Andy, who was away on a Boy Scout

Camping trip. She was worried that he would hear about

the accident from some other source.

"I'll go to the lobby and give his Scout Leader a call.

The boys are probably in bed at this time of night, but he

can tell him first thing in the morning". He then went to

the lobby to make that phone call. Five minutes later, he

rejoined the others in his wife's room. Edith could hardly

keep her eyes open but she did ask him about Andy. Trent

assured her that he was fine and asleep for the night and

suggested to Kelsey that maybe they should leave so Edith

could rest. Kelsey gave her Mom a hug and told her that

she loved her. Gabrielle also hugged her friend and all left the room with the exception of Trent, who stayed by his wife's side for a few more minutes. Edith took hold of his hand and expressed her concern for Joel. She hadn't mentioned it before because she didn't want Kelsey to fret.

"Honey, I don't want you to worry about Joel. Dr. Halloway said he's doing great and he wouldn't kid about something like that. He said Joel could come home in a few days after they did some tests. Honey, close your eyes and rest. You need to rest so you can come home in the morning". He kissed his wife tenderly and waited until her breathing told him she was asleep. Only then did he tiptoe outside the room to join the others. It was past midnight when they all left the hospital's parking lot. It had been a long and stressful evening.

CHAPTER 2

Edith Harmon was discharged from the hospital at noon the following day. As the doctor had predicted, every muscle in her body seem to hurt but she was very grateful to be alive and going home. She and Trent went to their son's room for a few minutes before having to leave for home. The doctor had just finished telling them that Joel would have to stay for at least a couple of days. The neurosurgeon wanted to make sure he hadn't missed anything when he read the x-ray. They were still worried about Joel's condition and were anxious to see him. So, they went in for a visit with Joel before leaving to go home. They were really surprised when Joel didn't object to staying in the hospital. They had expected him to argue, but Joel wasn't in a very talkative mood. Surprisingly, he seemed calm and resigned to stay those extra few days.

Joel's mind was so occupied that he only heard half of what his parents were saying to him. He didn't want to be rude but his mind kept wondering to whatever it was that kept happening to him. He couldn't tell anyone about it yet, not until he talked with Frisco.

He realized then that he was being rude and waved to his mom and dad as they started to leave the room and said to them, "I love you both, you know," hardly able to believe he had actually said those words. He hadn't told his parents he loved them for quite some time. It was childish to tell your parents you loved them, or so he thought.

"We love you too, Chestnut" they said, using the nickname he had come to dislike since becoming a teenager. It just wasn't cool to be called 'Chestnut' in front of his friends. He didn't mind Frisco hearing it because he was just like a brother to him. His mother blew him a kiss while his dad gave him the thumbs up. The door closed softly behind them leaving Joel with his disturbing thoughts.

Only Frisco would believe what Joel could hardly believe himself. His mom and dad would have thought there was something wrong with his head! That's why he had kept quiet about it. He didn't know what was happening, but he definitely knew what his mom and dad were going to say before they actually said the words aloud. It was really strange. No it was weird! He had to tell someone about it or he would explode! His mind was a jumble of thoughts when all of a sudden, he 'knew' someone was coming.

"Come in" he said. A surprised nurse opened the door, asking him how he knew she was standing at the door ready to knock.

"I just had a feeling you were there". Smiling, he

extended his arm for her to take a blood sample. Again, she looked at him in pure amazement.

"Are you sure you don't have E.S.P. or something young man?" He just shrugged and replied, "E.S.P? What does that mean exactly?"

"I think it means Extra Sensory Preception, I mean Perception or something of the sort. I've never paid too much attention to it, so I'm not sure. But it has something to do with being able to foresee stuff before it actually takes place."

"Oh yes?" replied Joel, looking at her intently. "That is very interesting. I'll have to read up on it. Nurse, I think the doctor wants you".

"You think so? If he did, he wouldn't know where to find me". She had barely finished saying those words when she heard, on the intercom, 'Nurse Smith, Dr. Halloway would like to speak to you in his office as soon as possible'.

"How did you know that?" she asked, looking at him strangely.

"Just a wild guess, that's all. Have a good day, Nurse Smith. Eh, I heard your name on the intercom besides seeing it on your name tag. I thought maybe you'd think I guessed it or something," he said stifling a giggle as she left his room.

Supper was surprisingly delicious considering the negative comments he'd heard about hospital food. Served on a colourful tray was a burger, mashed potatoes, pickles and cheese. A bottle of Coke as well as a pint of milk accompanied his supper along with a large chocolate chip muffin for desert. He ate every morsel on his plate and enjoyed it. 'It's almost like going to the restaurant' he thought. He was just pushing back his tray, when he heard in his head Frisco asking someone at the desk which room Joel was in. He hopped out of bed, opened the door and waited for Frisco to come round the corridor.

"Hi Buddy" he said as soon as Frisco reached his room.

"Hey man, what are you doing out of bed? Aren't you supposed to stay put?" Frisco asked in a worried tone.

Wincing, Joel replied "Yes, I'm supposed to stay put and yes, I'm sore all over but I knew you were coming and I wanted to surprise you."

"Sure, you knew I was coming. I told you I'd be here after supper. What were you gonna do, stand beside the door all night if I'd only shown up at 8 o'clock tonight? Get back in that bed you idiot, before the nurse or worse the doctor comes in."

"Don't worry, they're not coming. Frisco, you just wait till I tell you something that will probably freak you right out! But I swear it's the honest truth."

"What the heck are you talking about Joel? You sound awfully strange, are you feeling O.K.?" Frisco asked his friend, a bit worried. 'Maybe' he thought 'it's a concussion'. He had never seen anybody with a concussion, but he'd heard it made a person act differently. Walking into the room, Frisco hopped on one side of the hospital bed, leaving Joel still standing at the door, looking somewhat perturbed.

"Now Joel, calm down and tell me what you mean. You know I'm your friend and I promise I won't freak out".

"You promise"?

"Yes Joel, I promise. Come on, jump in".

Very slowly, Joel walked back to his bed and threw himself on top of the covers. Then slowly, he began to speak. "Last night, something really strange happened to me. I barely remember you and Kelsey coming in at Fundy Health Center before I blanked out. All of a sudden, there was something like a flash of light only brighter, and then I was floating; first in the room, then over the ambulance when all went blank. Once more I began floating but I found myself in a different place. I could hear voices all around me and I could see people bent over me. The flash of light appeared again, but this time it became a whirlwind that was drawing me to its center."

"My God Joel! Are you O.K. buddy?"

"I'm fine, but listen to this; I remember being frightened out of my wits when a voice or rather a whisper told me not to be scared. Just hearing that voice, I became very calm. For what seemed like hours I followed the voice through a tunnel of light, yes Frisco, a tunnel of light, that's the only way I can describe it. It was so beautiful I didn't want to ever leave it when suddenly; this beautiful soft voice told me to go back, that it was way too early for me. I became very confused because I desperately wanted to follow that light, so I refused and asked 'why was it too early?' But, he coaxed me back until I turned around and started going the opposite way".

"HE?" Frisco asked. "How did you know it was a 'he' if you didn't see anyone"?

Joel, still lost in his memories, looked at his friend and

answered; "You're right, I didn't see anyone but Frisco, I honestly believe I was in the presence of God."

Frisco was staring at his friend, trying to make sense of it all. He had heard about near death experiences, but he'd never spoken with anyone who had experienced it firsthand.

"Joel, if you say this is what happened to you, I believe it. It's just taken me by surprise. I've heard of such encounters, but I didn't know if it was actually true."

"Oh yes Frisco, it's true, but there's more."

"More! What more could there be?" In disbelief, Frisco asked his friend "Tell me everything Joel. What else is there"?

"You know, me being behind the door when you came in"?

"Yes Joel, go on."

"I knew you were on your way to my room. I was waiting for you. That's why I went to open the door."

"What do you mean, you 'knew'"?

"That's exactly what I mean Frisco, I know things before they actually happen. Not a long time beforehand, only a minute or so. Like right now, the nurse is coming, don't say a word."

Thirty seconds later, in comes Nurse Smith, smiling and holding a syringe.

"Oh no, not again! I don't hurt that much, I don't want another needle."

"Sorry! It's the doctor's order, turn on your side. And you young man" she said looking at Frisco, "if needles bother you, just turn your head the other way."

Frisco barely had time to turn his head when she announced: "Very good, it's done for another 6 hours. See you at 2 o'clock tomorrow morning."

"You mean you're going to wake me up in the middle of the night to give me a needle? That is really mean you know".

"I've been called worst things" she chuckled on her way out.

Frisco couldn't wait to resume their conversation. As soon as the door was closed behind Nurse Smith, he said: "Is there something else you haven't told me"?

"No that's it" Joel replied. "What do you think of me now? Are we still friends or am I too freaky for you"?

"Come on buddy, you know I'll always be your friend. And no, I don't think you're freaky at all. As a matter of fact, I think you must be pretty special. It's not everyone who gets a chance to experience the 'after life'.

"Is that what you think happened to me Frisco; that I died for a little while"? Frisco, who always had to analyze and make sense of everything, said, "My friend, there's a big possibility that this is exactly what took place. Dr. Halloway told us that they had lost your heartbeat completely for almost a full minute. Did you know that"?

"No, I did not know that! Why didn't the doctor tell me"?

"Well, give him a chance Joel, it only happened late last night. If your 'experiences' keep on happening, we'll find someone who will be able to help you deal with it. It must be kinda neat though, to be able to see things before it actually takes place."

"It's different, believe me" Joel replied, more than a little confused about the whole thing. "Do you really think that I was in God's presence last night Frisco? I really didn't want to come back. I didn't give a second thought to my family or even you Frisco. I just wanted to follow that amazingly soft voice and the beautiful light. It's really hard to explain, but now I'm glad that I did come back. I probably would have missed you, you big bully" he told his friend, giving him a slight punch on the shoulder.

"Yes buddy, I would have missed you too, a whole lot. We're much too young to die, aren't we?"

"That's for sure," Joel replied. "Now tell me what's happening in the village, anything interesting? Did you decide on a date for the prom yet"?

"Not quite," Frisco replied. "What about you? Did you

come up with someone yet? You always get the prettiest girls".

"Trouble with me is that I don't know if I should ask Holly or Kendra. Give me your honest opinion buddy. I need help in making such an important decision, if you know what I mean. I wouldn't want either one to get mad at me".

"I'm sure you'll ask the right one", Frisco said with a hint of mischief in his voice. Joel frowned and said: "What about you buddy?"

"Joel, what would you say if..." He didn't have a chance to finish his sentence when Joel jumped up; "Oh no! You're not asking Kelsey to accompany you to the prom. She's way too young to go on a date with you, especially to the graduation prom."

"How in the heck did you know I wanted to ask her?" he said with a look of disbelief on his face. "Never mind, of course you knew. Do you read people's mind, is that what happens?" Frisco asked, more annoyed than anything else. Joel sat on the bed again, looking dejected.

"I honestly don't know Frisco, it's really scary. I hope it goes away" he replied with a worried frown on his young face.

*****

Three days later, after a steady stream of clairvoyant moments, Joel was discharged from the Regional Hospital. For a long time no one but he and Frisco knew about the episodes that had taken place during his stay at the hospital. Nurse Smith was the only one who suspected something unusual, but didn't think it was anything that should be reported to the doctor.

Joel attended the prom with Holly and Frisco went with Kelsey. Joel still wasn't too happy that Kelsey was going as Frisco's date. His annoyance turned to surprise when his mom and dad agreed to it. His mom even helped

Kelsey get ready! They went shopping for a new dress and then she went for a fancy haircut. Girls!

The evening went by without mishap. There seemed to be a lapse to his psychic episodes which was fine with him. At this point, Frisco was still the only one that knew anything about it.

From the night of the graduation prom, Frisco and Kelsey became a couple. Kelsey finally asked Frisco why he had been ignoring her for so long. She asked him point blank why he had treated her the way he had. He explained to her that after he found himself physically attracted to her, he had to distance himself from her because she was still far too young to become involved with anyone. She accepted his explanation and they became inseparable. They were in love and nothing else mattered! That is why two month later a lot of tears were shed the day Frisco left for University to continue his studies. Kelsey was inconsolable. He promised he would be home for Christmas, if not Thanksgiving.

"But we're only in September. What am I going to do while you're gone"?

"I'll miss you too Kels, but you'll survive" he teased her. He knew it would be a long four months. Absence only made their hearts grow fonder. They would live for their school breaks.

Two years later, Kelsey followed him. By this time, they knew there would be no one else for either of them. The understanding was that as soon as both of them had received their diplomas, they would become husband and wife. And four years later, that is exactly what took place with the blessing of their families. Even Joel had come to terms with his sister marrying his best friend.

*****

Meanwhile, Joel finished his studies at a different university, majoring in philosophy. A course in extra sensitivity had been incorporated, at the suggestion of one of his professors. He was very much attuned to the supernatural. He was looked upon by his peers, as well as his teachers, as a person with unusual intuition and also somewhat religious in the fact that he attributed all of his psychic abilities to God, who he was convinced, he once had had a glimpse of. When one of his friends or a family member was in need of reassurance, Joel was able to help them because he seemed to know exactly what was troubling them. He certainly didn't brag about his abilities to see glimpses of the future, but he used it to help others 'if' and 'when' it was deemed necessary.

In University, he befriended a guy his own age who had moved from Western Canada after his parents had separated. For a whole year, Jacob talked about his dad and waited for him to show up; something which never happened. Joel could sense that he was progressively becoming depressed and at one point was even contemplating suicide, so one day he confronted him with it. Jacob admitted that he sometimes wished he was dead because his own father didn't even want to see him. Joel encouraged him to seek the help of a professional because he knew this was a serious matter. Jacob's survival instinct was very weak and almost at the breaking point. He knew this could happen because he had just finished reading a scientific report on survival instinct. That same evening, he encouraged Jacob to talk about all that was troubling him. During one of those talks Joel found out his friend had been blaming himself for his parent's break-up, so he suggested that Jacob talk to his mother and find out if she felt the same way.

"The only way I'll talk to her about this is if you come home with me. You can make her understand Joel, please"? It was a plea, more than just a request. Joel agreed to go and that night, they made plans to pay Jacob's mom a visit. She lived only a few hours away and Jacob went home every other weekend anyway. But she was surprised to see him come through the door. After introducing Joel and making small talk for an hour or so, Jacob told his mother he had something to ask her and if she didn't mind, he would like Joel to stay in the room. She assured him that it was fine.

Jacob's mom was shocked to hear that he was blaming himself for the separation. "I want you to promise me you will never think that again. You had absolutely nothing to do with what happened between me and your dad. It makes me realize it was wrong not to keep in touch with him. Things are going to change. I will try to locate him immediately. I'm very sorry about this Jacob, I never realized how much it bothered you". She walked over and hugged him close and told him how much she loved him, tears falling down her cheeks.

"I'm sorry Mom; I didn't mean to hurt your feelings".

"Sush, my feelings aren't hurt. I'm just glad you have such a good friend who encouraged you to tell me. I love you more than anything Jacob, I want you to always remember that O. K."?

"I will Mom, I love you too".

With Joel's support and encouragement, as well as a few visits to a good counselor, Jacob turned his way of thinking in another direction. He finally let go of his guilt and accepted the fact that it was not his fault his parents had broken up. He and his mom developed a closer relationship. On one of his weekend visit, she said, "Maybe your father didn't know where we were. It's entirely possible that this is the reason he didn't come for a visit. I'm getting closer to finding him. I was talking to his sister, your Aunt Mabel, and she gave me an address. Be patient a little while longer, we'll find him".

And find him she did. It wasn't easy for her to do this because there were still a lot of hurt feelings, but they reached an agreement. Jacob's father agreed to phone and talk to Jacob once a week and someday, when they were both ready, he would come for a visit. This is the way it went for almost two years. He and Jacob learned a lot about each other during those phone calls. Jacob's grades went up and Joel could see a huge difference in his friend.

There were definitely no more negative thoughts going through Jacob's mind. The time went by rather fast.

He received his diploma along with Joel and all his classmates. His Mom was beaming with pride and out of the corner of his eye, Jacob caught a glimpse of someone sitting next to her, someone whom he hadn't seen in almost three years! Joel had noticed the two walking in together and 'sensed' it was Jacob's dad. He glanced toward his friend and gave him thumbs up. The smile on Jacob's face was all Joel needed to make his day perfect. His own family was in attendance, which included Frisco and Kelsey, who were now a pair, his brother Andy who seemed to have grown up overnight and his mom and dad. They were all very proud of him as he accepted his diploma from his professor.

At the reception Jacob, visibly anxious to be alone with his dad, introduced Joel's family to his mom and dad. In the past couple of years, the Harmon's had grown fond of Jacob and the feeling was mutual. They knew of the situation with his father and were very glad to hear about the reunion.

A couple of days before that, Joel had attended Frisco's graduation at another University. He too received his diploma. He was on his way to become a renowned psychiatrist while Joel would be drawn in a completely different direction.

CHAPTER 3

10 Years Later

On the front door of a large building in the city of Saint John, New Brunswick, the letters F. J. O'Brien, Doctor of Psychiatry were displayed in large, bronze markings. Francis Joseph O'Brien, known as Frisco, was now an established doctor of the mind and very happily married to Kelsey Harmon.

Across the same city, people were lined up outside the Imperial Theater, waiting to be ushered in to see the most popular clairvoyant known in the area. Joel was now known as J.D. Harmon and had become very famous. Each one was secretly hoping to be chosen for a demonstration of J.D. Harmon's remarkable skills as a Psychic. Tickets had been sold out months ahead and J.D.'s manager, Tom Aicken, was beginning to sweat. Suppose too many tickets had been sold for the seating capacity of this theater. It was filling up fast and a quick peek outside told him his fears were about to be realized. The only possible solution would be to regretfully tell the people waiting in line that another show was scheduled for the following evening. He may as well start counting the remaining seats and tell the ushers to cut off the line. It was his job to tell the fans the disappointing news.

One of those disappointed fans, a young woman, told him she wouldn't be able to afford paying for a baby-sitter two evenings in a row. He asked her how much she'd need to be able to attend the following evening and handed her the amount. The same thing had happened on a previous occasion and he'd been advised by J.D. himself to do this.

It had cost J.D. big bucks, but obviously he thought it was worth it. As he had put it-- "What is a few hundred dollars if it means keeping the fans happy"?

This time, there were even more young mothers standing in line and once the word was out about the baby-sitting money, four more young moms came forward to claim the same amount.

Ten minutes before the show was to begin, Tom Aicken walked up to the front of the theatre and disappeared behind the curtain on the left side of the stage. Behind that curtain was the door that led to J.D.'s sitting room. J. D. seemed relaxed and smiled briefly when Tom informed him what had just taken place outside.

"You mean it's a full house tonight"?

"Yes sir, it is".

"Good, I'm getting a lot of vibes tonight. It must be a rather young audience, I can feel the energy" J.D. replied offhandedly.

"You've got that right", Tom answered as if they were

talking about the weather. "I would say about 75% are under 30 years of age." Tom, who was in his mid forties, was only now realizing how young 30 really was. He touched the top of his balding head, sneaked a look in the mirror and just shrugged his shoulders.

J.D. gave his friend a gentle push and said, "No Tom, you don't look old, you just look mature. There's a big difference you know."

"J.D., you stop looking inside my head. A guy can't even think when he's around you."

"Now Tom, you know me better than that. You're just as easy to read as an open book."

"Oh yea? I'll bet I am," Tom muttered to himself, looking at his watch. "You have five minutes left before you go on stage. Are you ready"?

"Don't I look ready"?

Tom looked at him in amazement. "Aren't you ever the least little bit nervous Joel Harmon?"

"Nope" was the only reply that came out of him.

*****

In the front row of the Imperial Theater, J.D.'s brother-in-law, Frisco and his wife Kelsey were softly whispering to each other. The two of them were as much in love now as they'd been over ten years ago. What their parents had thought to be 'puppy love' had turned out to be something much more lasting. Frisco and Kelsey were now the proud parents of a three year old daughter Alexandra and a ten month old baby boy Sebastian. She was still on maternity leave and was thinking of taking a leave of absence for another year. She enjoyed being a stay at home mom! Dr. Francis O'Brien was still Frisco to his family and his close friends as J.D. Harmon was still Joel to his.

Joel stepped on stage as soon as the curtains opened. The audience stood up and started to clap before he had a chance to open his mouth. To quiet them, he lifted his arms and finally, the noise subsided.

"Good evening ladies and gentlemen. I'm really flattered to see so many of you here tonight. I hope I will keep up to your expectations. My name is J.D. Harmon and as much as I'd like to meet all of you personally, I'm sure you realize that this is not possible. One thing I can assure you of is this; one day, we will all meet personally in that special place which some of you call heaven, others call it paradise and again, some call it the 'after-life'. I'm here tonight to tell you there is no doubt in my mind that such a place exists".

"How can you be so sure Mr. Harmon"? Someone shouted from the back row. "I know because I've had a glimpse of it myself, more than a glimpse actually. It was such a beautiful a place that I didn't want to leave it and I honestly didn't want to come back. But I was made to understand that I had to return to my human condition and to my home and family. What I wanted to do more than anything was to follow the loving voice, the breathtaking light and the overwhelming presence of goodness that I can only call God."

After that statement, you could have heard a pin drop in the Imperial Theatre. There was complete silence as J.D. Harmon bowed his head for a few minutes. Then, he asked if there was a person in the audience who might have had a similar experience and whose name began with the letter D. Everyone's attention turned to a young woman halfway to the back who was slowly getting up from her seat.

"May I ask your name Miss?" J.D. asked her softly while someone offered her a microphone.

"Danelle Anderson. And yes Mr. Harmon, I experienced what you've just described, about a year ago."

"Would you like to share your experience with our audience"?

"Yes, I would" she replied.

"Tom, would you please escort our guest up on stage"?

"Certainly, Sir" he replied.

Once Danelle was standing beside J. D., she went on, "Like you, I didn't want to return to my physical, earthly body. It was the hardest decision I have ever had to make. After I entered the tunnel of light, I saw the most breathtaking golden city imaginable!"

"That is very interesting Miss Anderson, but please, go on, for I'm sure the audience is anxious to hear more".

"A beautiful being took my hand and made me understand that it was not the right time for me to come, that I had to return right away. I argued that he must be mistaken, that I was ready, begging him or her to let me go further. I began to weep as the being of light gently persuaded me to return to my body. I wasn't forced to return and I understood the decision was mine to make. All the same, the heavenly being helped me make the decision to return. I remember everything up to the moment my spirit or soul hovered over the hospital bed that held my lifeless body".

"Why were you in that condition Miss Anderson?"

"I had suffered a brain aneurysm and my parents had been told by the doctors to expect the worst. They thought it was unlikely that I would survive. You can imagine their amazement and joy when I opened my eyes and spoke a few words. My body felt so heavy and sadness filled my whole being. But then, seeing my parents cry with joy at my being alive, I understood why I had made the decision to come back".

Looking at the people sitting in the theater, Danelle shook her head and offered her apology for having gone on so long. To her amazement, some of the people had tears streaming down their faces.

"Thank you so much for sharing that with us Danelle. I do believe that life as we know it is but a mirror reflection of the life that is to come. Maybe there is someone else with us who might have had a similar experience"? But the audience remained quiet and Tom escorted Miss Anderson back to her seat.

J. D. Harmon resumed his performance, which delighted and entertained his many fans.

CHAPTER 4

In his office, Dr. Francis O'Brien had just returned from his lunch hour. His next appointment was with a young man named Connor Harrigan. This was a case so unique that he didn't know how he was going to handle it. While on his lunch hour, he had come to a decision that he hoped would be in the best interest of his young patient. During their previous session, Connor had revealed to him that he would often leave his body and wonder to unknown places. Frisco knew that this boy was very bright; therefore he wasn't questioning his intelligence. The extensive tests he had performed revealed that Connor had a very high I.Q.

He didn't like to admit that this session would have to be the last. Doctor O'Brien had no explanation for these out of body experiences. It was out of his league, so to speak. There was only one person he knew of who might be able to help Connor deal with this dilemma.

This person was his long time friend Joel, known as J.D. Harmon, the most respected clairvoyant in the country. The decision would depend on how Connor would react to his suggestion.

He was still deep in thoughts when there was a light tap on his office door. Getting up from behind his desk, he opened the door and welcomed Connor in, inviting him to sit down. Connor swung himself into the nearest chair.

"How have you been keeping since our last appointment Connor"?

"The same, Doctor" was his only reply but his body language told a different story. He sat as if he were sitting on pins and needles. Dr. O'Brien thought he looked very nervous today.

'What could have happened to affect him this way?' he wondered. He was trying to figure out Connor's actions and it wasn't easy. This case wasn't his ordinary, everyday patient analogy case. There was something about Connor Harrigan that he just couldn't put his finger on.

"Did something out of the ordinary happened to you in the past two weeks Connor, since our last appointment"?

"Kind of," Connor replied, looking embarrassed.

"Explain to me, in your own words, what took place to make you think it may have been out of the ordinary"?

Connor jumped up from his chair as if it were on fire, started pacing back and forth in front of the desk and all at once, he blurted out, "I think I was walking on the moon".

Being used to hearing almost anything from his patients, Dr. O'Brien wasn't shocked and gently asked, "You think, then you're not sure?"

"Well, I remember sitting on a park bench, looking up and admiring the full moon last Wednesday when all of a sudden, I left my body there on the bench and started flying really, really fast. It was faster than flying, I just can't explain it." Connor seemed hesitant for a moment and Dr. O'Brien encouraged him to go on.

"All of a sudden," he continued, I was way past the clouds and I could see the moon getting bigger and bigger. Then, my feet touched down on something that felt like sand. It wasn't like when the astronauts were on the moon. They just floated and seemed weightless, but I was walking like I'm doing here in this room. I looked around me and it was so bare. Nothing, there was nothing anywhere! Believe me, I was scared, really scared, so I shut my eyes and said, 'I wish I was back home.' Instantly, I was swept from that barren place which I assume was the moon and began flying again or whatever it was that I was doing. In no time at all, I was back on that bench, looking at the same moon but it was much prettier from the earth than it was when I was standing on the actual thing. Do you think I'm crazy Doctor? I beg you; please help me find out what's wrong with me".

Connor was speaking so fast he was out of breath. Dr. O'Brien lifted his right hand and asked Connor to please sit down again and relax. This time it was he who got up, walked over to where Connor was sitting and said; "First of all, you are not crazy, of this I can assure you. But you do experience things that not many human beings have or ever will experience. It is called 'Bi-Location' meaning you can be at two different locations at the same time. You can also travel as fast as you can think. There is one other person I know of, who has experienced this phenomenon. He was known as 'le Cure d'Ar.' Did you ever hear of him by any chance?"

"No, I haven't, but I'm glad I'm not the only one. I don't want it to happen again. Can you do something to keep it from happening Dr."?

"I don't think so Connor, but I do know someone, a

friend of mine actually, who may be able to help. Do you know what a clairvoyant or a psychic is"?

Timidly, Connor answered that yes, he thought he knew. "Is it someone who can read minds or see the future"?

"Something like that, yes. Like you, he is very special. He has abilities that very few human beings have. How would you feel if I made an appointment to meet with him soon? Although it's against my better judgement, I think it would be worthwhile to go" he added, muttering to himself. Connor had heard the comment but didn't understand what it meant.

With renewed hope, Connor answered, "I wouldn't mind going at all. Maybe he'll be able to help me, because I sure do need help. I can't go on like this much longer".

"This is what I'll do then. I'll give this friend of mine a call and explain your case. I'll call you first thing tomorrow morning to let you know when and where you can meet with him. Are you O.K. with that"?

"Yes, I think so", Connor replied.

"In the meantime, keep your feelings low- keyed. In other words, don't wish for anything you don't really want" Dr. O'Brien said, tapping him lightly on the shoulder.

"O.K. Dr., that sounds easy enough. Thank you for seeing me on such short notice, but I really needed to talk to someone and I couldn't tell just anyone about what happened to me".

"Of course Connor, I understand your concern. Have a good afternoon and I'll get back to you as soon as I can tomorrow morning".

Dr. O'Brien stood up and escorted his young patient out, frowning as he closed the door and returned to his desk, hoping it wasn't too late to help this young man. As promised, he called Joel that evening and set up an appointment with Connor for the following day. It was now out of his hands although it wasn't his usual, professional way of dealing with difficult cases. He would have liked to resolve this case on his own. At least Connor would have someone to confide in and Frisco knew that Joel would do his best to help him. First thing the next morning, he

phoned Connor with the time and place for his meeting

with Joel. And Joel couldn't wait to meet this young man.

What an opportunity for him!

CHAPTER 5

Joel Harmon dialed the number he had often dialed in the past. At the end of the second ring, Kelsey answered.

"Hi Kelsey, how is my favorite sister?"

"Favorite sister, eh? Can't you come up with something more original than that Joel?" she playfully retorted.

"Now Kelsey, don't be nasty. How about if I said: 'how is my best friend's wife' instead. Could I get more original than that?"

"Joel, you are hopeless! Your favorite sister alias your best friend's wife is doing just fine. How about you? You sound as if you have something up your sleeve. Am I correct?"

"Well, sort of."

"Come on, spill it out."

"I just have a favour to ask of Frisco. I may as well come clean, I thought if I came to you first, there would be a better chance of him saying yes to my proposal".

"Well, at least you're honest about it. What is it?"

"You know that I'm having a Psychic Adventure Night next Friday evening, which is being held at Fundy High in St. George?"

"Of course I know. How could I forget when everyone I meet on the street is talking about it".

"Well, I need someone with a head on his shoulders, let's say someone on the other side of psychic".

"And", Kelsey finished for him, "you think my husband, your best friend may be that person. Am I correct?"

"Yes you are. How in the world could you have known that"?

"I guess I must have inherited some of my brother's abilities but tell me dear brother, what makes you think that Frisco may be unwilling to comply"?

"Because, I'm going to have to hypnotize him and you know how he feels about those things".

"I certainly do," Kelsey said, taking a deep breath. "Maybe and I mean 'maybe', if there is a good enough reason to do it, I might be able to persuade him to accept your 'invitation'. How good is your reason"?

"It concerns one of his former patients, as a matter of fact, one that Frisco all but begged me to see".

"He did?" Kelsey was surprised to hear that.

Joel continued, "Doesn't that prove something? Do you suppose that deep inside, Frisco agrees that not everything can be scientifically explained? If I can show this former patient of his that a psychiatrist can be made to regress in time, maybe I'll be able to make him understand that it's also possible to be foregressed into the future. Because that is what's actually happening to his ex-patient, except neither he or Connor knows it yet".

"Hem, sounds complicated to me but I'll do my best and let you know his answer tomorrow. You did say it was this coming Friday, didn't you"?

"That's correct and thanks a lot Kelsey. I don't know what I'd do without you".

"Tell me this Joel, what makes you so sure that this regressing and foregressing is possible? It isn't an everyday occurrence you know".

"Let me put it this way Kelsey; when we are born, we possess incredible abilities but shortly after birth, most of us lose these abilities except for very few, how could I put it, a few 'chosen ones'. Another few re-acquire some of these abilities after unusual circumstances, such as a heavy blow on the head or a near death experience, such as what happened to me. There's a very thin veil between life here on earth and eternal life, the life that is awaiting us after we die. A lot of people believe that dying is the end of living when in reality, dying is only the end of a very restricted life and the beginning of something awesome. Do I make sense Kelsey"?

"You make a lot of sense, as usual. I wish I was more like you. The only 'sense' that I have is a sense of humor I guess."

"Come now, we all love you just the way you are. Have a good day and I'll be waiting to hear from you tomorrow."

"Bye Joel," Kelsey said.

"Give my love to Alexandra and Sebastian," Joel said before he hung up the phone. He really had to start visiting his niece and nephew more often. All of a sudden, he felt the empty spot of longing inside his chest. He loved kids and someday, he hoped to have some of his own.

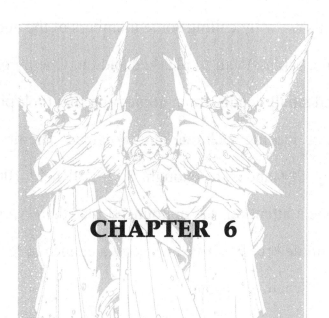

CHAPTER 6

Connor Harrigan was seated in the front row of the auditorium at Fundy High where Joel was having his Psychic Adventure Night. J.D. Harmon had made arrangements for Connor and Danelle to attend this special session as well as a very distinguished guest, a psychiatrist by the name of Dr. Francis O'Brien. The place was packed as usual. Tom Aiken went to the dressing room, advising Joel to be ready for appearance in 10 minutes.

"Thanks Tom, I'll be right along".

After having been introduced, which was needless, for everyone in Canada knew of the famous J.D. Harmon, Joel began his show by calling some members of the audience by name, asking them to please stand up. One by one, he revealed small details about something that took place in their past, leaving each one dumbfounded. The first hour went by fast and sure enough, J.D. still held 100% of everyone's attention. He announced that there would be a ten minute break to give everyone a chance to leave the room for whatever reason.

Once back on stage, he asked his three guests to join him. Reluctantly, Frisco followed Connor and Danelle Anderson up the steps leading to the stage area. Once J.D. had introduced each of them, he asked Frisco to take the chair opposite him. He then asked Frisco if he was in agreement to be brought into a hypnotic state, to which he answered, yes he was.

"Very well then, we'll begin. At the count of three, you will close your eyes, relax and go back in time." In a soothing voice, J.D. began to count, " one, two, three. Now Francis, I want you to go back specifically to the summer you turned 17 years old, just before your graduation. What can you tell me about that summer Francis"?

In a voice that sounded much younger than his 30 years, Dr. O'Brien replied, "I'm waiting for my friend Joel. He's coming to meet me so we can talk about the graduation dance. I'm throwing rocks in the water and I'm still waiting. Where is he, I wonder? I hope he didn't forget we were supposed to meet here after his appointment".

"Francis, do you know why Joel is unable to meet you on time"?

"No" was his only reply. Suddenly, he opened his eyes wide and became agitated.

"It's O.K. Francis, take your time. What do you remember"?

"It's Kelsey. She's getting out of the car and she's crying".

"Why is she crying Francis, do you remember"?

"There has been a car accident. Her Mom and Joel are both in the hospital". Again Francis became agitated.

"But they're O.K. aren't they"?

"Yes, they are!" Francis seemed to instantly relax.

"Now let's go forward by 24 hours. Where are you now Francis"?

"I'm in the hospital room with my friend Joel" he replied, smiling.

"Why are you happy today Francis?" J.D. questioned him.

"I'm so glad Joel is going to be all right. Last night, the doctor said he almost died, that his heart stopped for almost a minute. But today, he's just the same old Joel, thank goodness."

"Do you by any chance, notice something different with Joel today"?

"Well, yes, sort of. It's all a bit strange. He seems to know things before they actually happen".

"Is there anything else you witnessed that day Francis"?

"He told me that he was pulled into a tunnel of light, that

he heard a beautiful voice and felt a presence so powerful that he didn't want to leave it".

"Did he really? Did he say anything else by any chance"?

"Not really, well, except that he claimed to have met God that day, you know," Francis said in amazement.

"And what about you Francis, do you believe that Joel experienced God's presence, that he did meet God that day"?

Francis O'Brien readily agreed that yes, he had to believe it because Joel was so convincing.

"He and I are going to deal with it. He's my friend and I won't let him worry about it".

"That is very generous of you. At the count of three, you will not remember this conversation. 'One, two, three.'" J.D. flicked his fingers and Dr. O'Brien gave a little cough as if nothing had taken place.

"Thank you, Dr. O'Brien for your time".

"You're most welcome, Mr. Harmon" he replied, an amused look on his face.

J.D. Harmon stood in front of his audience and announced; "Dear friends, you have just witnessed a regression. Do you know who this Joel is that Dr. O'Brien was referring to under hypnosis? It was I, Joel David Harmon at age 17. Dr. Francis O'Brien was and still is my best friend Frisco".

To say the least, his fans were left baffled and they wanted to hear more. So, he continued, "If a person can be regressed in time, who's to say that a person cannot be foregressed or presaged into the future? I think it's very possible and tonight, for the first time ever, I am happy to present to you Connor Harrigan who has agreed to be, so to speak,' my guinea pig'. Is this correct Connor"?

"Yes sir, I'm willing to do it" Connor replied timidly.

"Please take a seat beside Dr. O'Brien. By the way, do you know this man"?

"Sure, he's my psychiatrist. I saw him only a couple of weeks ago".

"Interesting! Now we'll begin. At the count of three, your mind will no longer be here but somewhere in the future. There is nothing to be nervous about. I won't let anything happen to you, so just relax. 'One, two, three', where are you Connor"?

After only a moment's hesitation, Connor confidently replied, "I'm in Paris, France."

"How do you happen to be in that country Connor"?

"I come here anytime I please," he replied smiling.

"You do? Do you take the plane or the bus or do you drive"?

"Oh no, I just wish I was here or anywhere for that matter, and I find myself exactly where I want to be".

"This is very interesting Connor. What year is this anyway"?

"Why would you ask such a strange question. We're in

the year 2039 of course". "Smiling at his audience, J.D. said: "How silly of me not to remember what year it is!""

Dr. O'Brien couldn't believe his ears! So this was the reason Joel wanted both him and Connor here at the same time. And this was why he, as a psychiatrist, wasn't able to help Connor. This phenomenon, known as foregressing or presaging, had not yet been proven. Dr. O'Brien had to force his thoughts back to the present as Joel continued; "From where you are right now Connor, we'll go back 30 years to the year 2009, to be exact. Can you tell us what happened to you that year Connor"?

"That's the year I went to the moon and it scared the wits out of me!"

"Do you want to tell us about it"?

"Sure! I was just sitting on a park bench admiring the full moon, wishing I could walk on it when all of a sudden; I was flying very fast toward it. In a matter of seconds, I was standing on what I 'thought' was the moon, only to find out it wasn't such a nice place after all. I was very disappointed and said to myself that I wished I was back home. At the speed of light, I returned to my body, still sitting on that bench. Can you understand why I thought I was crazy?" Connor asked J.D., his eyes opened wide.

"I can see why you would think that. But you don't believe that now, do you? What happened to make you change your mind"?

"It was my doctor, Dr. O'Brien. He assured me that I wasn't crazy. He made arrangements for me to see Mr. J. D. Harmon, who explained to me what was taking place. I was told that I had special abilities".

"I see. At the count of three, you will not remember this conversation".

He then counted to three and Connor came out of his trance-like condition, not remembering anything of what had just taken place.

"Thank you Connor for being so helpful in showing our audience that there is such a thing as foregressing or presaging".

For the second time, the audience stood up, applauding loudly. To appease them, J. D. lifted his arms up and said, "I've kept the best for last. I present to you Miss Danelle Anderson".

Taking Danelle's hand, he led her to the other chair beside Connor Harrigan, facing Dr. O'Brien. Turning to his audience he said, "All of you must know something about E.S.P. or you wouldn't be here. Simply put, someone who can foretell future events, often brought on by near death experience, is known to have Extrasensory Perception; someone such as Miss Anderson and myself. Danelle suffered a brain aneurysm and was put on life support for several hours. Amazingly, she recuperated much faster than any of her doctors had predicted. For those of you who attended my last psychic session, you know what Danelle experienced. Much like myself, she went through the 'tunnel of light.' What I want to prove today is that this has really happened to her and was not just a figment of her imagination. Are you ready Miss Anderson"?

"Yes Mr. Harmon, I'm ready".

"At the count of three you will be back in the same hospital bed where you were once put on life support. One, two, three." Danelle's face seemed to suddenly change.

"What do you see, Danelle?" J. D. Harmon asked her softly.

"I'm not in my body. I'm looking down at the doctors and at Mom and Dad who are gathered around my bed. Mom and Dad are so sad. Why are they so sad"?

"You have to tell us, Danelle. We don't know either. What brought on their sadness"?

"Because I'm dying, that's why! Oh, I see a beautiful light and there's someone, an angel I think, waiting for me in the light. I follow him, he's so beautiful! We travel very fast when all of a sudden, I see a beautiful city just outside the light. I am drawn to that city; I want to go so badly." After that last statement, Danelle started to cry like a child.

"It's O.K. Danelle, I'm with you. Tell me, why can't you go to that beautiful city"?

"Because someone, with a voice like I've never heard before, is telling me that I can't go, not yet. I can't see him or her, but I can feel It's presence. I begged to stay, but the voice convinces me to go back. 'There is a time for everything' the voice is saying. The same angel I saw before is now beside me, telling me that I have to believe it. It's only because I'm loved so much that I have to return to my body. Finally, I agreed". Danelle begins to cry again.

"Why are you so sad Danelle"?

"I feel such a sense of loss!" Suddenly, she stops crying and says, "We're now going the opposite way. The angel is helping me along when all at once, I'm looking down at my lifeless body and the angel departs, but I now understand why I had to return. One reason is my parents. The other is realizing at that moment, that I hadn't yet accomplished what I was born to do".

"Relax now Danelle. At the count of three, you will

open your eyes and not remember this conversation. One, two, three." Danelle looked from one to the other and asked: "Is it over?"

"Yes my dear, it's over and you've done marvelously".

The audience was too stunned to react. It took a full 30 seconds before they got up to give Danelle a standing ovation. All she could do was wipe her eyes. She knew she was crying, but didn't know why.

After everyone was seated, J.D. Harmon stood up and thanked his audience, then he went on to thank his three guests before he said something that took a lot of them by surprise.

"We are all born with extraordinary abilities, but soon after our birth, these abilities are taken away from us, the direct result of Adam and Eve's fall or disobedience. Instead, we are given a strong survival instinct. While some of us regain some of these special abilities after undergoing near death experience, others come upon them by other means along their life's journey. Although it rarely happens, very few retain their extraordinary abilities as they grow older.

Sadly, some people develop a weak survival instinct, and these are the ones that feel their life is useless and consider committing suicide. They have a feeling that they don't belong in this world. Without a strong and healthy survival instinct, every human being would feel this way. If anyone of you or anyone you know confides in you that they have suicidal thoughts, don't hesitate to find someone like Dr. O'Brien to help you. He will strengthen your survival instinct and like Danelle was told, there is a time for everything. It is not our decision to make as to when our life on earth is over. But there is one thing I can assure you of; if you are kind, compassionate and forgiving, you will find more in the great city of light. On the other hand, if you are mean, judgmental and unforgiving, you will find less waiting for you in a city that is dimly lit. Goodnight and may God bless each and every one of you".

The curtains came down. The show was over and J. D. Harmon was more popular than ever.

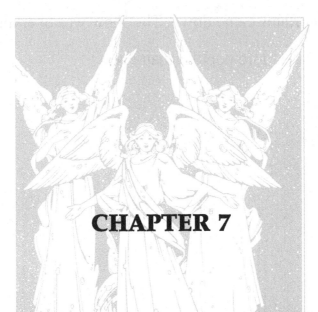

CHAPTER 7

Joel Harmon rushed to his dressing room, loosened his tie and asked Tom if he could possibly go and try to find Danelle before she disappeared in the crowd.

"Tell Miss Anderson that I would like to have a word with her". "Sure boss" Tom replied as he was hurrying out the door. He disappeared in a flash in the pursuit of Miss Anderson.

Ten minutes later he was back, followed by a puzzled Danelle. Joel met them at the door and apologized to Danelle for sending Tom after her instead of going himself.

"I knew it would be almost impossible to get to you in

time. Between autographs and hand shaking, I'd have lost you in the crowd. Hope you don't mind".

"Of course not, Mr. Harmon".

"Before we go any further, no more calling me 'Mr. Harmon'. From now on, I'm Joel to you, O. K.?"

"Sure, if that's what you prefer".

"I prefer," Joel answered with a smile. At that moment, Danelle thought he must be the most handsome man she had ever met. It made her blush that he was smiling and looking at her this way!

"What are you doing tomorrow evening"?

'Come now, Danelle, unfreeze,' she scolded herself. What had he just finished asking her? "Pardon me, I didn't get that".

"Are you busy tomorrow evening Danelle"?

"Eh, no, I don't think so. Are you having another session tomorrow night and want me to appear again as a guest"?

"No, I don't. I have three weeks until my next show".

"Oh, I see," she said looking down at the floor when

suddenly she knew what he wanted to ask her. The next few minutes flashed in front of her. She lifted her eyes to meet his and they both smiled as she answered, "Yes, I'll have dinner with you tomorrow night".

"Wow!" Joel exclaimed, not believing his ears. "I never thought I'd meet someone just like me, but you are, aren't you"?

"I suppose I am. Does it bother you"?

"Not at all, I'll just have to watch my thoughts when I'm around you", he said jokingly. Now he was beginning to understand Tom's comment from way back.

"Where shall we meet for dinner then"?

"Give me your address and I'll pick you up at six tomorrow evening. Is there any food you can't eat"?

"None that I know of, and I'm not a fussy eater. When I'm hungry any food looks appealing".

"Good, I'll surprise you then. Thanks for accepting my invitation on such short notice. By the way, is there someone special in your life, like a boyfriend or something"?

"Or something, eh? The answer is no, there isn't anyone of that description. I'll see you tomorrow then," she said, walking out of the room.

"Wait, I'll walk you to your car," Joel said, as he fell in step with her brisk walk.

*****

At six o'clock sharp the following day, Joel was ringing Danelle's doorbell. Taking a deep breath, she went to answer the door. She was running late for it had taken her over an hour choosing the right dress and another hour to do her hair. She had put her hair up with a clip only to brush it back down and then, swept it up again. As she was opening the door, she wondered if Joel would like her hair up. She received her answer when Joel let out a whistle and said, "I definitely like your hair that way. You look stunning with your hair up"!

A little flustered by his comment, Danelle mumbled, "Oh? Thanks, I don't wear it like this very often."

"Then, I'm glad you decided to wear it like that tonight. Joel just grinned and extended his hand to her, leading her to his blue Toyota Camry where he opened the passenger door for her in a gentlemanly fashion. Once in the car, they exchanged comments about the weather and about their day's activities. The time it took to drive to the restaurant seemed to be very short. They were remarkably comfortable with each other.

Joel had chosen a beautiful old European Restaurant that had been recommended to him by Frisco after he had taken Kelsey there on their anniversary. The dimly lit tables were very romantic as well as impressive. An ice bucket sat on the center of a table elegantly set for two. It had been a long time since Danelle had dined in such a luxurious place. She'd been more apt to eat from fast food take-outs than in fancy restaurants.

She and Joel shared an enjoyable meal served with

delectable wine. Conversation flowed as easily as the vintage wine they were enjoying. At twenty-eight years old, Danelle had had her share of male companionship but nothing serious had ever developed. The same was true for Joel. No one had yet captured his interest for any length of time. Yet, after only a few hours with this woman, he was mesmerized in a way that surprised him. Music beckoned them to dance. Anticipation sang an intoxicating melody in Joel's mind as he put his arms around her. Danger whispered a siren's song in Danelle's ear as she looked into his eyes. A kaleidoscope of senses is the only way to describe their first dance!

When the music stopped, Joel led Danelle to their table.

"Did I mention how beautiful you look tonight"?

"You're very kind, thank you".

"By the glances from the men in this room, I'm not the only one who thinks so. They can eat their heart out though, because I'm the one who has you sitting at my table".

"You're hilarious! But I'll admit that a girl likes to be appreciated".

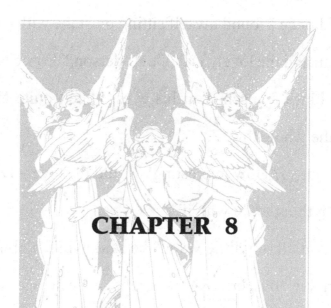

CHAPTER 8

Kelsey and Frisco were relaxing in front of the television after the children had been tucked in bed for the night. They always allowed a good hour for getting them ready for bed. This included a bedtime snack followed by brushing of teeth. It was a ritual that was rarely broken.

"We didn't have a chance to talk last night," Kelsey told Frisco. "Did you mind very much being hypnotized by Joel? I was a bit uneasy at first, knowing how you felt about it and I certainly don't blame you. I must be the biggest skeptic there is!"

"Amazingly, it didn't bother me as much as I thought

it would once I found myself sitting on stage with Connor Harrigan and the lovely Danelle Anderson," Frisco replied with a hint of mischief in his eyes. "I felt quite at ease about the whole thing".

"Is that so? How interesting! Would the lovely Danelle have anything to do with it"?

"Not at all, my little vixen" he said, while nibbling on her earlobe, "but seriously, being the one who had advised Connor to see Joel, I couldn't help feeling relieved that maybe there was hope for young Connor. As much as I hate to admit it, there are things one has no explanation for. What conclusion did you reach Kelsey"?

"If you want to know the truth, I thought this business about going into the future was a little farfetched. Do you, by any chance, happen to agree with Joel? Do you really believe that is what took place on the stage last night? That this Connor person was experiencing something that will actually take place thirty years from now"?

"As much as I hate to admit it, yes I think it's entirely

possible that this is what took place. The psyche has no limit. We place limits only because we don't know how to deal with certain things, things like Connor first experienced, thinking he was loosing his mind because he was experiencing something ordinary people do not. We tend to set limits on what we assume is possible and what isn't. Last night, Joel showed his audience that these barriers, under the right circumstances, can be eliminated. And why are you looking at me like that"?

"Like what"?

"You know what I mean. Do I detect a touch of mockery in those lovely eyes"?

"Now, would I, Kelsey O'Brien, dare to make fun of my husband"?

"Yes, you would. You wouldn't think twice about it and you know it. That's why I love you so much. You were always so easy to read, even in your early teens". Frisco pulled her close.

"Don't remind me of those days Frisco! I was a miserable human being and you had everything to do with it." Kelsey enjoyed rubbing that in once in a while. Frisco pulled her closer.

"Darling, that was the only way I knew to handle a situation in which I had no control over." He still cringed at what the outcome could have been if he hadn't sought the advice of his High School councilor, Mrs. Cromwell. She had encouraged him to ask Kelsey to the prom if he felt that strongly about it, but only after he had confided to her his dilemma concerning his best friend's sister.

Kelsey responded by hugging him back.

"We've gotten a little off track, didn't we? So, tell me Frisco, are you glad you complied and appeared as a guest of J. D. Harmon, my famous brother"?

"For everyone concerned, yes I'm glad I agreed to go. It proved that it is possible to reach into the future as well as go back into the past. It's a new awareness for me as much as it was for a lot of people last night. Did you hear the reaction of the audience? I can't wait to see the front page of the newspaper. The interest will certainly run high".

"My, my," Kelsey replied, stretching like a kitten in front of the fireplace. "I never thought I'd see the day when my husband and my brother would see eye to eye where matters of the mind are concerned. I can't wait to tell Mom and Dad about it. They've always been a little concerned since the two of you grew up and spread your wings in such opposite directions. But I think all is well, don't you agree"?

"Your brother and I have always agreed to disagree, if you know what I mean".

"Of course, I understand you, complicated husband of mine. When you and Joel have a difference of opinion, I never know what to believe. Some things will never change"!

With surprising strength, she pulled him to his feet, leading him toward their bedroom to retire for the night.

Frisco was being led like a lamb and he loved every minute of it.

CHAPTER 9

The morning paper's front page covered J. D. Harmon's story exclusively. In bold capital letters, this is what was printed; 'How would you like to be brought spontaneously into the future? It is now possible, according to J. D. Harmon, the famous clairvoyant.' The media was convinced they had put their fingers on something that was sure to sell, which proved to be true.

As word got around, the newspaper stand emptied as fast as they could be filled. Groups of people could be heard discussing the latest news. Could there be any truth to this statement or was it a clever plot for the newspaper company to sell its product?

As the day wore on, it became apparent that a lot of people believed that it could be true. Some of the people who had attended the previous night's performance told their friends and family what they had witnessed. For the next few days, it became the talk of the town. Therefore, it didn't take long for the news to get around.

Joel's next performance was scheduled to take place three weeks before Christmas. Tom had tried to discourage him from holding it in December fearing the show would be a flop with so many people busy shopping and attending get-togethers. But Joel had been insistent.

"It's the perfect time" was how he put it when Tom brought it up. Usually, he left all those decisions to his agent, but this time he felt strongly about holding his show at that particular time of year. And so, the preparations began.

On November 15th, posters went up followed by

newspaper advertisements and radio announcements. In the past, television broadcasters had declined J. D's request for a two minute Ad. This time, the local cable T.V. contacted him and offered him as much time as he wanted. National television stations were all but begging him to have his show broadcasted live. Apparently, news had gotten around big time!

"What do you think Tom? I know this is what we've wanted in the past, but do you really think it's a good idea to go on live television"?

"To be honest with you, I fear this could only mean one thing; someone out there wants to prove you wrong. What other reason could they have"?

"I really don't have a good feeling about this offer. I honestly think we should decline".

"Just let me know what you've decided and I'll take care of it".

"Maybe Danelle can help me make up my mind; I'll give her a call." As he sat looking at the telephone, his thoughts roamed to Danelle and their relationship. He and Danelle had been seeing each other regularly for the past couple of months. They enjoyed each other's company and respected each other's opinions. He would have to discuss this matter with her and see what she thought. He decided to call her immediately. She picked up on the first ring.

"Hi Sweets, how are you?"Joel asked her.

" I'm a whole lot better after hearing your voice. I was just sitting here thinking about you when the phone rang. How about that"?

"Why do I think you're pulling my leg"?

"Because I am," Danelle replied, giggling. "I was actually on my way out the door so I grabbed the phone in the hallway. Now, tell me your dilemma, because it must be serious for you to be calling at this time of day. Did you break a front tooth or something"?

"No, I didn't break any of my teeth and stop making fun of me. It is serious though, and it's something I think you should hear. Which way were you heading"?

"I could be heading your way, all you have to do is ask. I am, or rather I was on my way to the gym but it can wait. I'll see you in ten minutes".

"Don't keep me waiting," Joel replied in a devilish tone.

Danelle hung up the phone and laughed out loud. She couldn't wait to see him. She really liked that man. Her heart did a summersault as the realization set in that she not only liked that man, she loved him! And that made her stop abruptly with her hand still gripping the doorknob. Why hadn't she realized that sooner?

Ten minutes later as promised, Danelle was knocking on Joel's door.

"Come in, it's unlocked," Joel shouted from the dining room. As Danelle entered the room, Joel's eyes met hers and something incredible registered in his brain, something that almost knocked him off his chair. She stopped and Joel got up, their eye contact never breaking. All Joel said was "Danelle" and she knew what was to follow.

"I love you Danelle Anderson".

"I love you too Joel Harmon," she whispered.

"Oh Danelle, I never knew love could jolt your insides this way. I think I'm going to faint."

"No you won't" she wanted to reply but couldn't. She walked into his outstretched arms. Too moved to reply, she blinked back happy tears from her eyes. Joel could feel the moisture in his own eyes as he wiped hers with his thumbs. He was in love for the first time in his life. He had dated a lot of girls and that's what they were, girls. Danelle was a woman, an exquisite pearl of a woman. He was the oyster and didn't want to part with his precious pearl. So intense were his feelings, he couldn't bare to let her go. He didn't realize he was hugging her so hard; he only wanted her to be an extension of himself.

"My God Joel, slow down. Talk about knocking the socks off my feet"!

Still feeling dizzy from the sudden realization that he'd

been struck by either a bolt of lightning or was it Cupid's arrow, he sat down again, pulling Danelle on his lap.

"I'm sorry honey; I'm just so overwhelmed with feelings".

"Honey, does this mean we're engaged?" she boldly asked him.

"If you're accepting sweet Danelle, we're engaged," after which he kissed her lovingly.

When Danelle was able to come up for air, she asked him: "Is this the reason you called me to come here or did you have an ulterior motive"?

"I did have an ulterior motive but I forgot what it was".

Jumping off his lap, Danelle became serious.

"Now, what was so important that I had to rush here at your beck and call, although I have to admit that it was worth it" she went on, blushing unashamedly.

"You are so cute when you blush," Joel said, taking hold of her hands and kissing both palms. "Sweets" he said, his favorite name for her, "I'd like your opinion on something. These past couple of weeks, we've been practically hounded by T.V. broadcasters wanting us to appear on television. I'd like to know how you feel about having the show being broadcasted live on T. V. I know it makes a lot of sense and that I should be grateful for their offer, but I have bad vibes about it".

Danelle looked at him intently, making sure she wasn't picking up on his negative thoughts. No, these were definitely her own thoughts and they were not affirmative thoughts. In other words, she had bad vibes about it also. Anyone would jump at the chance to have a T.V. audience, so what was going on here? She looked at him and said; "Don't do it Joel. I can't explain it right now but we'll work on it later".

"Thanks love, for confirming my sentiments," Joel replied, still holding her fingers close to his lips. Danelle could feel his breath dancing on the palm of her hands, driving her to madness.

"May I have my hands back"?

"Maybe." They laughed like two kids. The future looked very promising indeed!

CHAPTER 10

The theme for J.D.'s next Psychic Show was, 'To go where no one has gone before' and was scheduled to be held on December 5th at the Imperial Theatre in Saint John, NB. Tickets were sold in record time. Some of his fans were left disappointed at having missed out on their ticket purchase and expressed their discontentment by e-mail, phone or postal service which prompted Tom to approach J. D. about scheduling a second show for the following week on December 12th. It was a hard decision for Joel to make, but after discussing it with Danelle; he agreed to go ahead with it. Neither one of them liked the idea of all those disappointed fans.

The morning of December 5th, the day of J.D. Harmon's first December Show, began on a happy note. Since the day of their declaration of love, Joel and Danelle had been walking on clouds, so to speak. Happiness radiated from the couple and naturally, it reflected on anyone they came in contact with. Tom Aiken was one of these people. It certainly hadn't come as a surprise to Tom when J.D. had told him about his engagement to Danelle. He could see it coming since the night he was sent running to find the enchanting Miss Anderson, following her second appearance on J.D.'s show.

He congratulated him, patted him on the shoulder and on second thought, gave him a bear hug before he scurried off, whistling a happy tune.

A half hour before the show began, Tom noticed J.D. looking unusually nervous and somewhat apprehensive. Announcing his engagement to Danelle was certainly not the reason for his nervousness, so Tom asked him point blank what the problem was.

"I have to tell my audience something tonight that will be hard to comprehend, never the less, it's important that they be informed".

"And, are you going to tell me what it is or do I have to wait along with the audience to find out what's making you so nervous"?

"Sorry my friend, but you'll have to wait".

"If I didn't know you better, I'd be insulted" Tom replied, grinning from ear to ear for he knew this had to be good, damn good!

Checking to make sure his tie was on straight, J.D. instinctively knew this was going to be the most important show he'd ever host. He felt it in his bones.

After everyone was seated, a hush came over the audience. The lights dimmed and the curtains were drawn. As usual, to alert the audience that the show was about to begin, the sound of trumpet echoed through the Imperial

Theater. In his new white suit, black shirt and white tie, J.D. looked very handsome as well as a bit mysterious. Kelsey and Frisco were sitting in the second row along with his parents and younger brother Andy. Frisco's parents, the O'Briens, were also in attendance. Danelle and Tom were seated in the front row, a row also reserved for physically challenged people.

"Good evening, ladies and gentleman".

The audience just roared. In his impatience to deliver his first message, he didn't enjoy all this applause. Danelle had noticed this humble side and loved him all the more for it. When the clapping finally died down, J.D. told his eager fans that he had a special announcement to make. Not having a clue as to what that was, they could only guess and speculate as they could be seen whispering to one another.

He extended his hand for Danelle to join him on stage. Once she was by his side, he went down on one knee and presented her with an exquisite diamond ring. The audience went absolutely wild!

"Meet my fiancée, Danelle Anderson. From now on, Danelle and I will be side by side on the J. D. Harmon shows".

The audience didn't seem to have a problem with that. The lovely Danelle would only add to his presentations. Then, he asked his fans for their undivided attention. As he put it, "There's an important message that I want to give you tonight".

After brushing a hand over his eyebrows, he went on in his very distinctive voice; "A very small and I mean 'small' minority of all people on this earth possesses the ability to travel in time and in space at will, but none the less, it 'has' and it 'does' happen. What has never been proven up to now is that anyone willing to travel in time, may possibly do so with the help of someone like myself. Regressing in time has been accomplished for centuries while presaging into the future is something that a lot of people have never even heard of. Tonight, I want you to understand that this phenomenon is a God given talent and like any God given gift, it has to be developed and used not only for one's own good, but also for the good of others. It should certainly never be used to hurt anyone".

To which his fans shouted: "Yeah! Yeah!"

J.D. seemed to hesitate for a few seconds but a squeeze from Danelle's fingers was enough to give him the courage to go on.

"Is there anyone in this audience who would like to be foregressed or presaged into the future, meaning that under hypnosis, you could travel forward and experience presaging, the actual account taking place in six months, one, ten or more years in the future"?

He didn't have to wait long for a young man to stand up and shyly make his way up to the front. Tom Aiken escorted him to the stage area where J.D. and Danelle both shook hands with him.

"How are you tonight?" J.D. asked him casually. The young man seemed to instantly relax.

"Very well, thank you," he replied.

"Do you believe or have you ever had an experience in presaging, at any given time in your life"?

"Yes," the young man eagerly replied.

"First, please tell us your name".

"Jeremy".

"If you don't have any objections, would you also tell us your last name".

Someone in the audience softly chuckled.

"Melvin, it's Jeremy Melvin Sir," he answered.

"Danelle and I would like to welcome and thank you for agreeing to appear on our show tonight whose theme is; 'To go where no one has gone before'.

Once more, the delighted audience roared with applause.

"How did you come to attend tonight's show Jeremy?" J. D. asked.

When Jeremy gave him a questioning look, J.D. told him, "This is for the benefit of our fans Jeremy. I know and Danelle knows why you're here".

"I wouldn't have missed this show for anything Sir. I've attended all of them so far, but tonight I almost didn't make it." Looking down at his feet, he murmured; "I was gone somewhere and lost track of time".

"Well Jeremy, I'm glad you did make it and please call me J.D. Before we begin, I'll ask you to take a seat over there where Danelle and I will join you shortly".

Turning to his audience, J. D. said, "During my last performance, another young man by the name of Connor Harrigan was transported in time under hypnosis. Tonight, I want to prove to you that although it happens only in rare cases, a person may travel in time on their own, without the outside help of someone such as myself. You may call it 'self hypnosis', I rather call it 'self presaging'.

Anticipation could be felt coming from the members of the audience.

"First, I'll clarify how Jeremy and I first met. After witnessing Connor's travel in time, Jeremy contacted me. He, like Connor, didn't know what was happening to him, a feeling that can be very scary. I explained as best I could what was taking place when he found himself at different locations within minutes. It reassured him that he wasn't insane, but indeed very special. Following our meeting, Jeremy was convinced that by appearing on tonight's show, he could prevent others from suffering through the ridicule of their peers and help them deal with their extraordinary abilities. And I can't stress this enough, 'like any other abilities,' it has the potential to be harmful if it's not kept under control. Therefore, it is extremely important to tread carefully and to seek help when needed".

He and Danelle walked over, each taking a seat across from where Jeremy was seated, still looking somewhat nervous.

"We'll follow the same steps as we did at my house a couple of days ago. Are you O.K. with this Jeremy"?

"Yes Sir, I'm ready" Jeremy replied.

"Let's get on with it then. What happened tonight Jeremy, that you lost track of time"?

"I found myself somewhere else".

"Would you like to return to the same place if you could"?

"I sure would," he replied.

"Well then, relax for a minute and then go back to your destination".

Jeremy closed his eyes for about thirty seconds, and then reopened them only to stare straight ahead at nothing in particular. J.D. got up, took Danelle's hand and walked to the edge of the stage.

"You are now witnessing a presaging totally brought about by the individual himself, meaning without the help of another person. I did not hypnotize him, but only suggested that he relax. I can't tell you exactly how long he'll be gone, so let's get on with the show". Jeremy looked as if he was frozen in time.

J.D. then asked his audience "Is there a person sitting in the third back row, whose name begins with the letter E who has had to travel for hours to attend tonight's show"?

"Yes! Yes!" came a reply.

"Please come up on stage and introduce yourself'.

A young girl in her late teens came forward, her long dark hair flowing down to her waist.

"Care to tell us your name Miss?" J.D. prompted her.

"I'm Erika Latimer. How are you Mr. Harmon and you Miss Anderson?"

She could hardly keep still in her excitement to finally be able to meet the famous clairvoyant and his assistant.

"We're very well 'Thank you', and it's our pleasure to meet you Erika. May I ask where you're from"?

"I'm from Whitehorse, in the Yukon".

"Great! We have a person in our midst who is able to experience the magnificent view of the northern lights on a regular basis. Welcome to New Brunswick Erika. Do you mind telling the audience how old you are"?

"Certainly not. I'm eighteen years old and I'm honored to be appearing on your show Mr. Harmon. What you've said tonight and what I've read in the papers has been my beliefs since I was a very young child. That's the reason I've been saving my money to attend tonight's show".

"Any reason in particular, beside those you've just mentioned, that made you come to this decision"?

Erika looked at J.D. for a few seconds, her intelligent eyes dancing with expectation. She had waited a long time to tell her story. She was visibly anxious to finally be able to share it with someone who would understand what she was talking about.

"Go ahead Erika, tell us what it is that compelled you to save your money to come here tonight".

Looking down at her hands, she seemed hesitant, when all at once confidence lit her beautiful dark eyes.

"I've always been able to see and communicate with

angels. Like right now," she motioned with her hand, "they're here surrounding us with light." Everyone automatically looked up. "They tell me they're Guardian Angels and that there are trillions of them".

"You mean they're here now, among us?" Even J. D. seemed amazed. The audience was flabbergasted!

"Yes, they are. Whenever I have a problem that I feel I can't deal with, I ask them for advice and they always help me come to a decision. They are beautiful beings who accept and love me exactly the way I am. And they've assured me that they're always available to help any of us, if only we would ask. Did you ever see an angel Mr. Harmon?" she asked hopefully.

"Interesting question Erika, but first let me assure you that I believe what you have just told us. I sense that you are afraid of rejection. As for whether or not I'm able to see angels, I can tell you that I've experienced an awareness of what angels are like, but I have never seen one. My impression of angels is that they are beings of light that radiates happiness."

"That is exactly what they are Mr. Harmon"!

"The difference between you and I Erika, is that I've never been able to see angels when I'm awake and alert. I may be able to foresee future events but I can't see those Beings of Light in their spirit form the way you do. Erika, do you realize how special you are"?

'If you want to know the truth Mr. Harmon, I've thought for years that there must be something wrong with me. No one believed me when I told them I could see angels. Even Mom and Dad called them my 'imaginary friends' but they have since come to accept that I'm telling the truth. In early childhood, one of my aunts even suggested they bring me for psychiatric care. Another one said she was sure I was either possessed or that I had a brain tumor. Special you ask? It was more like having an inferiority complex!"

"I know Erika, how hard it can be for some of us to live

in our limited world, and our world is very limited. There are so many possibilities out there but people are afraid to explore. They are made to feel abnormal or in your case, inferior. I was fortunate that my family and my best friend accepted my so called 'strange behavior' without question. They were concerned about me, of course that I might have been left with brain damage following my car accident. But after being reassured by the best specialist in the hospital, they accepted the fact that I had received a special gift from Above . What happened to you Erika, to bring out your special gift"?

"Nothing, nothing at all. From as far back as I can remember, I have been able to see angels and communicate with them. I've always thought everyone else could see them too".

Still holding Erika's hand, J.D. addressed his audience: "Remarkable, don't you agree? If this eighteen year old girl can see and communicate with angels, and I'm convinced that she can, how many more people out there can do the same but are afraid to voice it"?

The entire audience roared with applause. Turning back to Erika, J. D. asked her if she believed there would come a day when most people would be able to communicate with angels. She replied: "I sure hope so Mr. Harmon. Thank you so much for having me on your show. My friends in Whitehorse will be so excited to hear about this"!

"The pleasure was ours Erika".

Danelle hugged her before she was escorted to her seat. This was the first time Erika had been able to express herself openly and it felt so good! Mr. Harmon and Miss Anderson believed her! She had been so worried that they wouldn't.

Silence reigned in the old Theatre for the next few minutes. Each time a revelation such as this took place; J. D. gave his audience some time to absorb it. In the meantime, he had something on his mind that Danelle had encouraged him to share with his fans. He could see that tonight was the perfect time to reveal it. This was a special audience he had tonight, he could feel their energy!

He wondered about the media and what would appear on the front page of tomorrow's paper but never the less, he went ahead. He had a gut feeling that these people would understand what he wanted to bring across. And Jeremy was going to help him accomplish that.

As if on cue, Jeremy turned his head sharply and looked at J. D. in amazement. J. D. walked over to where he had left Jeremy sitting comfortably for the past fifteen minutes. All through Erika's testimony, Jeremy had remained in his trancelike immobility.

"So Jeremy, did you have a good visit"?

"I sure did," he replied.

"Would you like to tell us where you went, who and what you saw"?

"I went to visit my cousin in Australia".

"And?" J. D. prompted him.

"He showed me a lagoon with three crocodiles

sunbathing on the edge of the water. We didn't get too close because crocodiles do not like to be disturbed".

"Yes, that's what I understand. Can you tell us anything else that happened while you were there Jeremy"?

"We talked and sat on the beach for a long time. The sun was really hot, so hot I thought I was going to get sunburned. Mr. Harmon, I'm very confused. I don't understand how I was able to be in Australia a few minutes ago and now I'm here on your stage," he went on in a childlike voice.

"Jeremy, you have absolutely nothing to worry or to be confused about. Just relax while I explain to you and to the audience what actually took place right here on this stage in front of them". Turning to his fans, he said; "Dear people, with your own eyes you have witnessed what transpired a few minutes ago. Jeremy actually traveled into the future on his own, without the help of someone as myself or anyone else. Almost a century ago, there was a monk by the name of Le Cure d'Ars who was also able to travel in space and time on his own. He is now deceased and to my knowledge, Jeremy is now the only human being who is able to accomplish this. It doesn't mean that such a person doesn't exist; only that it's not known to me personally. I would love to hear from anyone who has information on any such a person".

Turning to Jeremy, he added: "Didn't I tell you that you were special Jeremy? Come here young man, I want to congratulate you". Both he and Danelle shook hands with Jeremy after which he was escorted to his seat amid all the applause.

J. D. had his audience's attention and he was going to use it to his best advantage.

"Have you ever wondered what it was like at the beginning of 'the big picture'? I have, and I'm sure at least some of you have wondered about it also. Some may even believe in the 'big bang' which, in my mind insults our intelligence. Never the less, you have the right to believe what you want. I choose to believe in a loving Creator".

"I believe that the first humans created by God were

able to do many things that are now out of reach for us. The first humans were so intelligent that they became what we call "smarty pants".

This comment brought a bout of laughter through the big Theatre. He continued; "those first humans became disobedient, wanting to do their own thing, so to speak. And, like any good parent must do, the Creator God had to discipline them. He had to put his disobedient children on 'time out' but not only that, he also had to take away some of their privileges, because they weren't using those privileges as they ought. Let me explain; we, the descendents of Adam and Eve are still able to see, to taste, to feel and to love, which is good; if we were without any of those abilities, we'd really miss them wouldn't we? Now, let me give you an example of what I mean by saying that God took away some of our privileges. For all parents in attendance here tonight, lets say your child is disobedient and you need to teach that child a lesson. Therefore, he or she would have to be disciplined in an effective way which only a good parent can do. The punishment could be something as simple as this; no dessert at the end of his meals for one week. The child would still be getting his meals regularly because you love that child and want what's best for his health and after all, desert is only an added bonus".

J. D. could see people nodding their heads in agreement, especially the parents.

"With this picture in mind, I've come to the conclusion that at one point in history, human beings had a lot more privileges than what we have at the present time. Some of those privileges may have included communicating with angels when they needed them, similar to what you've just heard Erika Latimer say. I also believe that those first humans may have been able to transport themselves in time like Jeremy Melvin and Connor Harrigan. Another possibility would have been the ability to heal their own bodies and those who were dear to them. Jesus was able to do all these things two thousand years ago, didn't he?

Why do you think Jesus was able to perform all those 'miracles'? I would guess that it was because he wasn't subject to the limitations of humankind, for he was the Son of God and was obedient to the end. He was an obedient Adam. There was simply no need for discipline, no need to take away his privileges".

J. D. could sense the interest that was being generated from his statement. He continued, taking a step forward toward his fans.

"Now, listen carefully to this, dear people. Any medical doctor can attest to the fact that our human brain does not function at its full capacity. Don't you find this rather interesting? Now again, concerning Jesus at the tender age of twelve, without education he was able to preach to his elders. To me, that's even more amazing than the miracles He performed during his adult life. All that knowledge had to be stored in His brain at the time he was born and stayed there as he grew up".

"Wow!" could be heard throughout the audience.

"What this fact tells me" J. D. continued, "is that some of our brain power has been taken away from us for being disobedient children. Adam and Eve represent the whole human race, therefore we share their punishment. God, being the loving Father that He is, is watching us carefully, and once He determines that our 'time out' has been effective, He will give us back all the freedom that was once ours, seemingly what the garden of Eden offered Adam and Eve and their offspring at the beginning of time. Of course, in earth time, this could take billions of years. Remember your old Bible teachings? "With God, one day is like a thousand years and a thousand years is like a day"? One million years could be a short period in eternity. Our small minds have a hard time comprehending these time lapses.

The message I aim at you tonight is that I firmly believe that one day, all of our privileges will be given back to us. We'll be able to do all the things we can only dream of doing in our present state, that of being on a 'time out' ".

Sounds of agreement were flowing through the crowd that evening as J.D. continued, "Someone recently asked me why we had to die. I was left dumfounded because I didn't have an answer. After reflecting on it, my answer to all is this : Dying, which really means ' releasing of the spirit from the restraining body', is necessary in order for us to be able to return to our source of greater joy, which is God, the Creator of all things".

J. D.'s audience was kept captive and not a sound was heard until he gave his final bow. Then, the applause resounded throughout the whole building.

"Thank you so much for your attentiveness. Until next time, live your life to the fullest and God bless"!

Whether or not they believed his message was now out of his hands. All he could do was deliver it and he believed God would take care of the rest.

Tom now understood J.D.'s apprehension before

the show. Joel had outdone himself tonight. His fans, himself included, had a lot to ponder and discuss during the coming days.

Chapter 11

There were only three days remaining until the December 12th performance. As predicted, the media had gotten hold of some of the people who were in attendance the week before. The whole country was buzzing with the fact that it had been so well documented. J. D. knew that he couldn't repeat the performance that had taken place the previous week because for one thing, Erika Latimer had returned home to Whitehorse. In the course of her conversation with him and Danelle, Erika had mentioned that she was boarding the plane early the following morning. It was time for J. D. to find new people if he wanted to keep the interest of his fans. With Danelle by his side, he felt very confident.

The very next day, J. D. received a telephone call from Frisco.

"Seems we never have time to get together anymore Joel" Frisco stated. "A shame really! As a matter of fact, the kids have been asking about you".

"Now I feel bad. I know I've been neglecting my precious niece and nephew. After this coming Thursday night, I'll make time for them on a regular basis like a good uncle should, I promise. I really do miss them. So, what's up, old buddy"?

"Oh, just something I thought you might be interested in, or I should say Kelsey thought you would be interested".

"How is my sister doing? Being the obedient wife, is she"?

"Obedient, my foot! She's being the same Kelsey she always was, headstrong and very outspoken. But then, that's the reason I married her. Talking about marriage, when are you and Danelle planning to tie the knot? The subject came up in our conversation last night. Kelsey thought a winter wedding would be very pretty. She also thinks Danelle is just waiting for you to agree on a date, is she right"?

"Now, what could possibly suggest that"?

"Well, you know how girls are when they get together, and they did meet at Tim Horton's a few days ago. Does that answer your question"?

"I suppose so. I think I hear wedding bells ringing. No, sorry, it's my doorbell. Hold on, I'll be right back".

While Joel was gone to see who was at the door, Frisco was deep in thoughts of his own. He was thinking about yesterday's appointment with a certain Mrs. Donovan. When he had mentioned it to Kelsey the previous night, she thought it would be a great idea to call Joel. It was one of those cases which Frisco just couldn't solve. Joel's voice brought him back to reality.

"I'm back, Frisco. What were you saying before we got side-tracked to weddings"?

"Ah yes, something I wouldn't likely forget! I've had the visit of a young mother of twin girls yesterday. She seemed very concerned because her daughters claim they can talk and communicate with animals".

"Yes, continue," Joel said when Frisco sounded hesitant.

"From my observation, the girls seemed to be very intelligent but are convinced that they can understand animal talk or whatever it is that they do. It was amazing to listen to them, but as a psychiatrist, I couldn't reassure the mother that it was normal behavior. The twins are happy and can't understand why their mom and dad are so concerned. Kelsey and I thought you'd be interested to hear about them".

"Interested? Frisco old boy, you're the answer to my prayers! I've been searching for someone like that ever since I read about Francis of Assisi, a monk who lived in the twelve century. Among other things, he could communicate with animals too. He is sometimes portrayed feeding birds and speaking to them, as well as preaching to the fish jumping out of the sea to listen to his sermons. When do you think I could meet these girls"?

'Well, thought Frisco, I have my answer. I guess he's interested', although he didn't have a clue what Joel was talking about. Aloud he said: "I suppose it's up to the parents. Is there a day that would be more convenient for you"?

"Let me see, today is Tuesday and lets assume they're genuine, I'd love to have them appear as my guests on Thursday night, my last Psychic Show of the season. Do you think I could call the parents? I'd like to meet with them as soon as possible".

"As a matter of fact, I've already suggested it to the mother, but I told her I had to get in touch with you first. She was very enthusiastic about meeting you, the famous

J. D. Harmon, I must say! Under these circumstances, I think it would be O.K. to contact her".

"Give me their name and phone number".

"Just a second, I have it down on a piece of paper".

"I hope her husband is home too because I want to get the ball rolling. And, tell Kelsey she'll be the first to know when we have a date for the wedding. Don't forget or she'll be upset".

"I wouldn't likely forget! Kelsey will remind me as soon as I walk through the door tonight. Thank you, Joel, for agreeing to see Mrs. Donovan. Her name is Michele and her husband's name is Randy. The twins are Monica, spelled M-o-n-i-c-a, and Emily. They're real cuties".

"How old are they"?

"They just had their twelfth birthday. Let me know how you made out O.K.?"

"That's the least I can do for you Frisco my friend. I really appreciate the fact that you've thought of me. Maybe

you and Kelsey can plan to attend Thursday night's show.
No hypnosis this time, I promise".

"Maybe, I'll talk to your sister about it. Talk to you
soon, bye".

"Sure, and give my love to Alexandra and Sebastian. I
promise we'll go see them soon".

CHAPTER 12

As soon as Joel hung up the phone, he dialed the Donovan's number; when a woman answered, Joel introduced himself.

"Oh, hello Mr. Harmon, my husband and I were hoping to hear from you". He could hear the girls in the background asking their mother if it was J. D. Harmon on the phone, to which the woman tried to muffle their voices with her hand on the receiver.

"I'm calling to tell you how much I would like to interview your two young daughters. Is this possible"?

"When Dr. O'Brien called to suggest a meeting with

you, the girls were overjoyed. I don't think they realize how concerned we are about them. We thought they should have outgrown this 'make believe' stage by now. My husband and I have discussed it and he agrees that we should meet with you if you're interested and if you think you can help. When would it be convenient for you Mr. Harmon"?

"Any time that it's convenient for you and the sooner the better. I'd like to meet with the four of you as soon as possible".

"Well, let me see, my husband will be home at 4:30 and I could have supper ready then. We could probably meet you around six this evening if that gives you enough time to prepare".

"You bet it does! I can't wait to meet those girls." He could hear giggles in the background. "Here is my address. Do you mind if my assistant attends this meeting?"

"Do you mean that lovely woman I saw standing beside you in the picture on the front page of the paper"?

"That would be Danelle, yes".

"Then, of course we don't mind. The twins are so excited to meet both you and Danelle in person".

"It's settled then, we'll see you all at six".

J. D. couldn't believe his luck! Lately, individuals with special abilities seemed to be popping up from every direction. He had yet to see for himself how these two young girls could communicate with animals. Interesting!

Next, he had to call Danelle and ask her if she'd be able to attend the meeting. Hopefully, she hadn't made other plans.

She answered on the second ring and assured him she wouldn't miss this meeting for the world. Before they hung up, Joel said; "Remind me to ask you something before you leave tonight will you? I don't want to forget it".

"You devil you, Joel Harmon. You're going to keep me in suspense, aren't you? You can be sure I won't let you off the hook. See you in a few hours. I'll be there at five with some food. Anything special you would like to have for supper"?

"No, but keep it light. I'm too anxious to eat much".

"O.K., I love you".

"Love you too".

Danelle arrived with tuna salad, crusty rolls and fruit cups for desert. Joel dropped a couple of tea bags in two cups and poured boiling water over it. "Thank you to whoever invented the tea bag," he said.

"I wonder who it was." Danelle couldn't help saying.

After their modest meal was consumed, they still had about thirty minutes to spare so they each took turns going in to brush their teeth while waiting for the Donovan family to arrive. They 'accidentally' bumped into each other which resulted in a hugging session.

"Thank you Danelle for coming on such short notice. You always manage to ease my anxieties. I don't know what I'd do without you Sweets".

"I'm sure you'd manage". She went on to give him a

neck message which brutally ended with the sound of the doorbell.

"They're here!" Joel exclaimed. "Thank you for taking the knots out of my neck. I'll return the favour later".

Straightening his tie, he rushed to the door to greet the young family. After inviting them in, he introduced them to Danelle.

Michele Donovan introduced her husband Randy before introducing the twins and then herself. Monica and Emily were just beaming as Joel and Danelle shook their hands in turn, asking them if they wanted a glass of soda pop, which the girls accepted gracefully.

Danelle couldn't resist the urge to comment: "My, don't the two of you look alike! How does your Mom and Dad tell you apart?"

"Oh, it's easy" both said at the same time, "she's the ugly one" each pointing at the other, laughing.

"O.K. now, both of you look me straight in the eyes and tell me your names".

"I'm Emily" the first one said, "and I'm Monica" said the other one. Danelle shook her head no saying, "I think your pulling my leg. I think YOU are Monica and YOU are Emily".

The girls looked at each other and then at their parents in amazement and exclaimed; "How did you know"?

"I have my ways. I was once a kid myself, so that makes me an expert. Now, make yourselves comfy".

Taking a sip of their soft drink, the girls followed Danelle to the sitting room with Joel and the Donovans in tow.

"Thank you Mr. and Mrs. Donovan for bringing the girls to meet us.

We're always looking for someone new to enhance our shows and I think we may have found them or rather, Dr. O'Brien found them. How do you feel about appearing as guests on the J.D. Harmon show girls? That is of course, if you pass the test and if your Mom and Dad agree".

Both heads turned expectantly toward their parents.

"Can we, please Mom, Dad"?

Their father was the first to answer, "First, let's hear what Mr. Harmon has to say, and then we'll decide".

Turning to Joel he asked, "Do you think that Monica and Emily have special gifts and are able to communicate with animals, as they claim they can?"

"It's entirely possible," Joel replied, "but until Danelle and I talk with them individually, I can't confirm or reject it, so lets get started. Danelle, will you take Emily to the living room while Monica and I go into the kitchen? Mr. and Mrs. Donovan, make yourselves comfortable. There are magazines on that table. This won't take very long".

'Of course, go ahead".

No more than ten minutes later, J.D. returned to the sitting room with Monica. Randy and Michele Donovan stood up, anxious to hear what had transpired.

"So, Mr. Harmon, what do you make of it?" Michele asked.

"I think," J. D. answered, "that you have exceptionally

gifted daughters. Let's wait for Danelle to come back with Emily".

Monica was just beaming with pride!

"Dad, Mr. Harmon said I was a natural and that his fans would love to hear what I have to say about the animals, or rather what the animals have to say to us".

"Is that so?"

"I hope Miss Anderson finds the same with Emily, because sometimes she's shy," Monica said. From the doorway, this statement came from Danelle as she and Emily re-entered the room. "I don't think you have anything to worry about Monica. Emily definitely has something wonderful to tell people on Thursday night. But we won't pressure you to agree Mr. and Mrs. Donovan. Let's discuss it at length." In agreement, Joel replied, "We most definitely won't pressure you."

After the four of them had discussed how the interview would be conducted, Joel said; "We will leave you to discuss this matter as a family while Danelle and I find something to do. Take all the time you need, just call us in when you're ready".

"O.K." the girls replied in unison, looking at their parents for approval. Michele and Randy took the initiative and asked the twins to please take a seat while

J. D. and Danelle retreated to the kitchen. Looking at the twins, their father asked, "Will you girls be on your best behavior 'if' we decide on a yes?"

"Yes, we will," both replied at the same time.

Now it was their mother's turn to question them.

"The show is taking place across the city, so we'll have to leave early. Will you finish your homework without complaining Thursday afternoon, with time to spare so you can get ready to leave at six o'clock that evening"?

"Yes, we will," replied both girls.

"Now," asked Randy, "do you know what will take place during the interview?"

"Mr. Harmon said he would ask us some questions"

replied Monica, "and all we had to do was answer truthfully."

"That's what Miss Anderson told me too," Emily went on. "She also said we should answer the questions plainly and not mumble so that people will understand what we say. We can do that, can't we Monica"?

"Of course we can, that's not hard to do at all".

Looking at his wife for approval, Randy continued as Michele nodded to him. "If you're both sure you want to do this, I guess we don't have any objections".

"Thank you Mom! Thank you Dad! Can we go tell Mr. Harmon and Danelle? She said we could call her by her first name," Emily added, noticing the look on her father's face.

"Go ahead, we'll wait here," he replied.

As the girls breezed out of the room, Randy looked at his wife and said; "I sure hope they know what they're doing and that we don't regret our decision."

"So do I," Michele replied.

They could hear laughter coming from the kitchen area. A few minutes later, they all reappeared, chatting away.

"Thank you so much Mr. and Mrs. Donovan, for agreeing to let Emily and Monica appear on our show. We can't tell you how much we appreciate it. And please, don't worry; no harm will come from this interview." Joel could sense their reluctance. "We'll let you go home now and get these two girls ready for bed. You don't want to be late for school tomorrow morning, do you girls"?

"No, we don't!" they replied.

"Be good and we will see you at the Imperial on Thursday evening, right"?

"Right!"

The door had hardly closed behind them when Danelle threw herself in Joel's arms. She was so excited; she could barely restrain herself from jumping up and down. "What impression did you get from Monica, Joel? Was it what you were expecting"?

"Yes, it was that and more. Did Emily fill you in on how they were doing their communicating"?

"She did. They don't hear animals say actual words or even make certain noise, but they hear it all inside their heads, by telepathy. They actually understand the needs of the animals. Isn't that amazing"?

"Amazing isn't a strong enough word to describe them. They're like two peas in a pod, what one feels, the other one feels also. Besides looking alike, they also think alike most of the time. But of course, they're two separate human beings, not clones. Identical twins are often found to glide on the same brain waves. I've never encountered anyone like them. I think we've hit the jackpot"!

"I think we may very well have honey. This is so exciting! So, what did you want me to remind you of tonight"?

"Now Danelle, don't pretend with me", Joel chuckled, "you know what I'm going to ask but you just want to torment me, don't you?"

"Your right, I do, but I want to hear the words come out of your mouth. What did you want to ask me Joel"?

"I can see that you're not going to make it easy for me, are you? It's like this; would you like to decide on a date for a certain wedding"?

"A wedding? Do you mean our wedding, Joel dear"?

"That would be the wedding I'm referring to".

'Well, let me think about it for a minute".

"That's O.K., it can wait, there's no hurry,"he teased her.

"Oh yes, there is! How about New Year's Eve? Is it acceptable to be married on New Year's Eve, do you think"?

"I have never heard such nonsense"!

"Oh,no? Well, I think it's the perfect date to get married. We become husband and wife and the next morning, it's a brand new year, full of expectations. Oh Joel, you are such a romantic"!

"And you, my love, are so easy to please. Really, I can't

wait for us to be married! The next three weeks will be the longest of my life. I love you Sweets and don't you ever forget it".

"As if I could," she whispered in his ear. Had she actually whispered those words or was it something else? He wasn't sure and it didn't matter!

CHAPTER 13

On the morning of Thursday, December 12th, the sky was overcast but the weather was mild. By mid-day, it was snowing heavily, huge fluffy snowflakes. The ground gradually became covered in a pure white blanket of snow. At about three o'clock that afternoon, the clouds dispersed and the sun appeared, leaving a clear blue sky.

In New Brunswick, the sun is extinguished very early on fall and winter nights, especially after the time change in late October. By six o'clock that evening, the stars illuminated the darkened sky.

The twins weren't used to going out after dark, especially

on school days. It was a big deal for them to get all dressed up for their appearance on the J. D. Harmon

Show. Homework had been finished in record time and they were on their best behavior. Being too anxious to eat much of their supper, their Mom and Dad understood because their own stomach felt a bit nervous too.

By six fifteen, they were all in the car, buckled up and ready to head for the Imperial Theatre. Joel and Danelle had instructed them by phone as to which entrance door to use so they wouldn't get caught amid the throng of people waiting in line to get in.

Tom hadn't yet met the twins but he had heard interesting things about them. Both J.D. and Danelle seemed very confident this morning that these two young girls would "make" the show, so to speak. He ushered the two girls and their parents in and made sure they were all comfortably seated in the very front row.

Michele Donovan immediately recognized Dr. O'Brien

sitting close by with his wife. She waved, reached across and introduced her husband Randy.

"Thank you so much Dr. O'Brien, for suggesting we bring the girls to meet with Mr. Harmon. It's taken a load off our shoulders".

"I'm glad it worked out." Looking at the twins he said, "You girls look very happy tonight." He winked at them and they both started giggling like typical twelve year olds.

Fans were steadily streaming in, right up to a few minutes before seven. With the usual sound of the trumpet, all noise subsided. The curtains were drawn and J. D. Harmon, with Danelle by his side, made their grand entrance followed by deafening applause.

As he did at the beginning of every performance, J. D. began to call out names of people, asking them if they'd like to come up on stage. Some refused, but most of them accepted. Taking each aside, he asked them permission to divulge certain personal information in public. Some responded negatively and he respected their wishes, at which point they exited the stage area and were escorted back to their seats. To the ones who stayed, he made revelations that left them and the audience speechless. His fans never seemed to tire of him and he was becoming more popular than ever.

An hour into the show, he announced to his audience that he had some very special guests to introduce to them. He motioned for Tom to assist the twins up on stage. The girls seemed very relaxed as he went on to introduce them as 'The Amazing Twins,' Monica and Emily Donovan.

Of course, when the audience heard 'Amazing Twins,' they knew they were in for a treat and responded accordingly.

Emily had automatically gone to stand beside Danelle while Monica had gone to J.D.'s side. They were just pulsating with anticipation and didn't seem to be the least bit nervous. As J.D. had predicted, the twins were undoubtedly naturals.

"Dear audience, this is Monica, an amazing twelve year old girl with very special abilities," he said, "and that is her twin sister Emily. They are able to communicate with the animal kingdom."

"Wow!" could be heard throughout the Theatre.

"And," he went on, emphasizing on his next statement; "This feat is accomplished by means of telepathy, meaning brainwave activities, opposed to spoken words". The appreciative audience applauded all the louder.

"Now girls, tell the audience what the animals have to say to us and especially to all who are attending tonight's show. First, let me ask you a question. Do you have a dog"?

"Yes, we do," they replied.

"Then, we'll start with him. O.K. Monica, explain to us what your dog says to you."

Monica took a deep breath before she answered; "Every morning, my dog tells me, inside my head, that he needs to go outside for a while. After I let him back in, he tells me that he's hungry. He also tells me often that he loves all of us, me and Emily, Mom and Dad. He also lets Emily and I know when he's too hot or too cold or when he's thirsty".

"That is very interesting. Thank you Monica".

Turning toward Danelle and Emily, J.D. said, "Now your turn."

"Emily dear, do you talk to any other animals beside your dog"?

Emily nodded her head. "Yes, we do".

"By the way, what is your dog's name"?

"It's Zack" Emily proudly replied.

"Great name! Now, beside Zack, what other animals do you communicate with"?

"Oh, there are lots of them! The week before Easter, we went to watch some deer in a large field and one of them got close to us. He told me, in my mind, that he loved running free in the woods. He also said that he likes eating green grass in the Spring, and a lot of other things".

"And, you can hear all that inside your head?" J.D. asked her.

"Yes, Mr. Harmon, I do", she answered.

J. D. then asked Monica if there was anything else she would like to pass on to the fans. She responded with a question.

"Why is it Mr. Harmon, that only Emily and I can hear the animals? Our friends say that we're just making it up, that animals don't talk. Even Mom and Dad can't hear them but they don't make fun of us".

"Monica," J.D. answered, "the reason your Mom and Dad, as well as most of the rest of humankind cannot "hear" the animals talk, is because we don't have the ability to do so, while you and Emily do. I can see that for the two of you, communicating with animals is as normal as anything else you do, but I can assure you that you are both very unique and very special. Did you ever hear the story of Francis of Assisi"?

"No," both answered at the same time.

"It's a true story which happened a long time ago and it goes like this. Francis was born into a rich family, having the same ability that you girls have. He was often ridiculed by some of his acquaintances for being seen talking to animals. . His parents knew that Francis was a special child, but way back then, people thought differently about such things as they do now, especially about something that couldn't be explained. Francis squandered a lot of his parent's money trying to get more friends but it didn't work. He went on to lead a lonely life, his only real friends being the animals. When he reached his early twenties, he decided to live away from everyone he knew. That is how he came to form an order of monks whom are known today as the

' Franciscans'. During that time, he was often portrayed as talking 'to' and 'with' the birds while feeding them. He grew to become a very Holy Man whose sermons were listened to not only by people, but also by the birds of the air and the wild animals of the forest. Even the fish came jumping out of the brooks and rivers to hear the Word of God. That tells you how special he was! Today, he is known as Saint Francis, the monk who wrote the popular prayer "Make me a channel of your peace, where there is hatred let me bring you love….."

"That is a nice story Mr. Harmon! We have never tried talking to the fish, have we Emily?" Monica said. "No," Emily replied, "but we talk with the birds a lot. They're thankful everyday for being able to fly and to find food."

"Oh yes", Monica piped up, "and also, they want to be our friends. Only, people are not aware of this. The birds are so glad Emily and I can understand them"!

"What about bears and wolves and all those scary animals? Did you ever communicate with any of those Monica"?

"We did, but we're very careful not to get too close. They are not as friendly as the deer but also, they're not as dangerous as some people seem to think they are. Their instinct is to attack when in danger and to be aggressive when they're hungry. They told us it's the only way they can survive, didn't they Emily"?

"Yes, they did," Emily replied "and we think they're very nice animals. Mom and Dad only allow us to visit and communicate with the wild animals at the zoo".

"That's a very good idea and thank you Emily and Monica for your information concerning the animals." J. D. then asked them if there was anything else they would like to say to the people.

"Yes, I do Mr. Harmon," Monica said, lifting her hand up as if she was in the classroom. "We have to be nice to all the animals, even the wild ones who realize that they've been put on this earth to provide food for humans as well as food for other animals. We should never abuse animals. Pets are very, very special, cats and dogs especially. They told me that they live to please their owners. Did you know this, Mr. Harmon"?

"I knew it but I wasn't 100% sure, and now I am. Thank you so much for giving us that information Monica. Just knowing that this is coming straight from the animals themselves is amazing! I'll bet you a lot of people didn't know these things. Am I right, members of this audience"? In answer, the delighted fans broke into applause.

"I have two more questions for you girls".

"Yes, Mr. Harmon, what is it"?

"Did you ever watch the movie Tarzan"?

"Yes we did, he's really cool"!

Turning to his fans, J.D. said; "Do you realize that these two girls are able to do the same thing as the legendary Tarzan did except, of course, they don't jump from tree to tree, do you girls"?

Laughing, they replied, "Mr. Harmon, we'd never do that."

"I know, I was only teasing. I'm curious about something else though. Can you also communicate with insects"?

Monica replied first. "Only the larger ones, like butterflies and bumblebees, and still it's hard to get through to them".

"We can hardly hear them," Emily commented. "Mostly, they're only interested in looking for nectar in the flowers. They're very smart though. Some of them come from far away to spend time with us, and then they return home without the help of anyone. I asked them how they knew which way to go and they told me they were guided by their natural instinct. Do you know what that means Mr. Harmon"?

'I think I know what it means" J. D. replied, winking at his audience.

"Thank you girls for informing us about what the animals expect from us.

"Yeah! Yeah!" The fans shouted. Danelle hugged both girls before Tom lead them back to their seats. It was time for intermission.

As the curtains closed, the twins waved at J. D. and Danelle as they were leaving the stage area for a short break.

*****

Upon returning for the second part of the show, Danelle and J.D. told their fans they had something to share with them. All eyes turned expectantly on them as J.D spoke first. "Danelle and I will be married in two weeks time, actually on New Year's Eve".

The clapping was so loud it was thunderous. The twins were jumping up

and down and had to be calmed by their parents. Kelsey and Frisco were giving them 'thumbs up'. Her brother was finally getting married and Kelsey couldn't be happier! It was time for Joel to settle down and start a family and Danelle was the perfect woman for him. Kelsey could already picture the winter wedding. It would be so pretty.

The show went on and at the end; Joel gave his final bow and said, "Until April, rest assured that God loves all his creatures, each and everyone of us, including the animals. Keep well while God keeps you in his care!"

Joel and Danelle exited from the stage area as the curtains slowly closed behind them one more time. At their next appearance in April, they'd be introducing themselves as Mr. and Mrs. Harmon.

CHAPTER 14

Joel and Danelle had a beautiful wedding celebration. Joel's little niece Alexandra, made a cute flower girl. Even little Sebastian was having fun. He laughed at everything his big sister did, whether it was funny or not.

Danelle's immediate family, her Mom and Dad and younger brother Shane, had arrived early that morning. Everyone was in a festive mood and Danelle was happy to have her family there. That was the one thing she missed; being away from her family. She hadn't seen them in a long while and promised herself she would go visit them more often.

It was on a beautiful moonlit and crisp New Year's Eve that they became husband and wife. Following the thirty minute ceremony, all of one hundred and seventy five friends and family members gathered for a reception at Fort Howe Restaurant. Among the invited guests were the Donovan family, Connor Harrigan and his mom, Jeremy Melvin and his girlfriend and Joel's manager and friend, Tom Aiken. They would have liked to see Erika Latimer attend too, but the traveling distance was too great to make it possible.

It was a memorable event that had been planned to a tee. The flower arrangements were astonishing, with poinsettias in abundance. Mistletoe was hung over every door and at every entry point. All decorations were an array of red and white with some green. Danelle's dress was pure white with a white fur-trimmed mantle. A white fur head band adorned her head which made her look like an angel!

Joel wore a black tuxedo with a white shirt, red cumber

bund and bow tie. His best man Frisco and the two ushers, Andy and Shane wore the same color. Danelle's Maid of Honour, Kelsey wore a red and white long sleeved dress and white fur hat while the two bride's maids, her dear friends and co-workers Mary and Nicole, wore red dresses with red head bands. It was a spectacular wedding and the bride and groom looked as happy as could be.

"Isn't Danelle the prettiest bride ever?" Emily asked her Mom. "I think you may be right, love," her mother replied. Monica, standing beside her Dad, discreetly whispered, "Did you think Mom was the prettiest bride when you married her, Dad?"

"There is no doubt in my mind, your Mom was the prettiest bride I've ever seen," replied her father. "That's what I thought," she answered, a big smile on her face.

Across the room, Frisco was remembering the day he and Kelsey had been married. He looked past the bride's maids, where Kelsey was standing, looking beautiful in her special gown. The years had been good to her. He winked to her and she gave him a smile that still had the power to melt his heart. Life was good; in fact 'Life was great'!

*****

The Harmon's six week honeymoon was spent in Brazil. Both had had a mutual yearning to go to Brazil, especially to Rio de Janeiro, so it had been easy to come to that decision. They didn't have any planned performances until the middle of April. Danelle didn't have to return to work until the end of February. They planned on returning home a week before the end of that month so that Danelle would have time to relax before returning to her demanding job as a Physical Education teacher. They also wanted plenty of time to visit with Joel's little niece and nephew, Alexandra and Sebastian, and to be able to visit with their parents and deliver their souvenirs in person. They would have lots of photos of great places to share with their friends. The world was full of wonders and they had made plans to witness at least a tiny bit if it!

During their stay in Brazil, they came upon a little village just outside Rio de Janeiro and while they were exploring the village, they spotted a little boy who seemed to be hiding behind a large tree. They approached him slowly, fearing he would run away. It became apparent that he couldn't speak English very well but he managed to say hello. He seemed to be afraid to say anymore than that, when a woman hurriedly came forward and tried to pull him away. Danelle spoke up. "Oh please, he isn't bothering us. We were the ones asking him questions. Are you his mother"?

"Si, me him mother." Shaking her head from side to side, she added, "Mohad not well, he speak to animals."

"Would you repeat that please?" Danelle spoke slowly. She had to repeat her sentence as the woman wasn't answering. All at once, she blurted out, "Mohad speak to animals, but he good boy." Needless to say, J.D. and Danelle were stunned by that statement.

"How old is he? What age is your son?" But the woman didn't reply. Then, the boy whispered something to his mother and she answered, "Eight", showing eight fingers while pulling her son closer to her. Apparently, Mohad could understand English to some extent, maybe even better than his mother.

A man, coming from the opposite direction, began to speak to them in fairly good English. He told them that the villagers made fun of Mohad because he was sometimes heard talking to animals and birds. He was being called a name equivalent to a weirdo, he stated.

No wonder the poor boy was trying to hide! The man was obviously not his father for when Danelle asked him what was being done to help Mohad deal with that abuse; he shook his head in a helpless manner and walked away.

Danelle couldn't help what she did next. She approached mother and son and gave them both a hug, telling Mohad he was a very special little boy, hoping he understood at least some of it. When she and Joel turned around to leave, they were rewarded by a smile from both Mohad and his mom.

In Canada, the twins were considered gifted because of their ability to communicate to animals, while in this small community in Brazil, they would have been ridiculed, the way Mohad was being made fun of by his peers. Joel hoped that one day, he might be able to do something to change the attitude of such people, but he was at a loss to know how he would come to achieve it. There seemed to be no solution at the moment.

Once in their hotel room, that's when he realized that television might be the only way to accomplish that. He knew he was well known across Canada, but that seemed to be the extent of his fame. A limited number of people from across the border into the U.S. had heard of him by word of mouth, or by reading newspaper articles, but that really wasn't much.

Joel and Danelle discussed it that evening and came to the conclusion that they had to expand their wings, so to speak. Their main concern was to educate people all over the world, not only in Canada, about what they had discovered. They made plans to accomplish this once they were back in Canada.

On their return home from their honeymoon, Joel decided to contact C.T.V.. He and Danelle paid a visit to Tom who, at first, was a little reluctant, but never the less he complied with J. D's wishes and contacted the office at C.T.V. For reasons unknown to Tom, C.T.V. accepted his proposal of a televised J.D. Harmon Show without question, as though he was doing them a favour. Deals were made and agreements were signed without delay. The televised show was scheduled for the end of April.

As usual, the Imperial Theatre in Saint John was packed, but there was also a distinct difference on the night of April 28[th.] Bright lights were shining on Joel and Danelle as they made their stage entrance, making it difficult for Joel to concentrate on his subjects.

Danelle held his hand tightly and whispered, "You'll get used to it, don't worry love, and just think of little Mohad".

"You're right, Sweets. I just hope I don't live to regret this decision".

J.D. tried his best to keep up a good front but he found it extremely difficult. His fans would not respond to something that was not spontaneous, plus he felt like a traitor for leading these people on a televised journey. To make it all worthwhile for his fans, he had to find it in him to make the best of this unfortunate situation, plus he had to remember the reason why they had come to this decision. The little boy from Brazil was never far from his or Danelle's thoughts.

His most recent guests were invited to attend this show because he realized he might not get a second chance to tell and show people around the globe about these people with incredible abilities. He also knew at this point, that another televised performance would not be repeated. No more T.V. cameras would shine in his face or in his guest's faces! Therefore, he had to give this show his all! Tonight, he had to come through for his fans. They had paid good money for what he was going to deliver and he wasn't going to let them down!

He returned Danelle's hand-squeeze and she nodded. Without having spoken one word, she understood his ultimate decision. No more cameras after tonight!

"Good evening, ladies and gentlemen. Welcome to our first psychic show in the New Year. My wife, Danelle, and I are thrilled to see so many of you here tonight. We have honestly missed you". At the mention of "wife" the whole audience applauded loudly.

"As you can see for yourselves, this show is different from all our previous ones. Never before has one of our performances been observed by so many people throughout the world as it will be tonight. From the beginning, I've always had a personal audience, the old fashion kind, you might say. But with today's technology, we had to take this opportunity to reach as many people as possible. There are some incredible people out there, in all parts of the world, with the ability to do unbelievable things. These are gifted people who are sometimes ridiculed, because they can achieve what some people perceive as 'impossible'. My dear people, these persons should be treated with respect. They should never be shunned or called names such as 'dunce' 'stupid' or 'freaks' ".

There was no doubt that he was holding his viewers attention as he went on; "During our honeymoon abroad, Danelle and I met a young boy and his mother. The boy, whose name was Mohad, was able to communicate with animals. Because no one understood what was actually happening with Mohad, they made fun of him to the point where he started hiding from people. When we first saw him, he was hiding behind a tree even with his mother close by. When we asked him his name, his mother rushed over and tried to pull him away from us. If it hadn't been for a man walking by, we would never have found out about his special ability. In fairly good English, the man told us that Mohad was often heard talking to birds and other animals and for that reason, people in his village were making fun of him and he had no friends to play with".

Danelle picked up where J. D. left off. "You can see why little Mohad felt that he had to hide from his people. I hope he took our advice and ignored the name calling. We tried to convince him and his mother that he was indeed a very gifted and special child and that he shouldn't be ashamed to talk to the birds or to any animals, but to be careful. We tried to explain to him and his mom that there were twin girls in Canada who could do the same. Whether or not they understood us, we're not sure. We can only hope that they did".

The clicking of cameras was the only noise to be heard until that last sentence. Then, the audience applauded for a long time. To silence them, J. D. brought his arms up, and then went on; "For this special televised performance, we've invited our most recent guests in the hope of drawing attention to those exceptionally talented persons who think they have to ignore their gifts in fear of being made fun of. Danelle will help to explain to you what I mean".

Taking a step forward, Danelle continued; "Tonight, extraordinary people can testify in front of our T.V. audience of over a million viewers, that certain things can happen for which there are no explanation. Some of you have already seen with your own eyes and heard with your own ears, happenings that we can only dream about. For example, did you know that J.D. only became a clairvoyant after he underwent a near death experience"?

"Danelle is also an example," Joel continued; "After suffering from a brain aneurysm, she like myself, can see glimpses of the future as well as pick up someone's thoughts for a couple of seconds. Contrary to some people's belief, we cannot 'read' people's minds".

"What I experienced and what Joel also experienced is

a glimpse of the 'after life', the presence of God and His angelic beings, while going through the so called 'tunnel of light' or the transition to the new life. After these events, we became aware of having certain abilities that we hadn't previously possessed".

"At this point, I'm asking all those people who have been invited to appear as guests on tonight's special show, to come forward and tell the world what they have discovered in the past six months." Danelle gestured for them to come up.

One by one, they came on stage, escorted by Tom. The first one to reach Danelle and J.D.'s side was Erika Latimer.

"Hello Erika. I'm glad you were able to make it back to Saint John, New Brunswick. Ladies and gentlemen, this young lady is Erika Latimer and she flew from Whitehorse, Yukon, to be with us tonight. Erika has the special ability to see and talk to angels, especially Guardian Angels".

"How have you been Erika?" Danelle asked her.

"I've been doing great! It's so good to see you again Mr. and Mrs. Harmon".

"We'll get right down to business Erika. Are you ready to confirm your previous statement concerning angels"?

"Absolutely, Mr. Harmon."

"You are still able to see angels and communicate with them, am I correct"?

"Yes you are. I have been in touch with them many times since our last meeting. They say it's good that people are coming to terms with this fact, because it will happen more frequently in the future. They want us all to know that we have nothing to fear from them, that their only purpose in existing is to praise God and to help the human race. That is what God created them for. If we were to call on them more often, our lives would be far less complicated. And we should submit to the will of the Creator, because only then will we be truly happy. A lot of people presently think that they can manage on their own, without divine help, but soon they will come to realize that it's impossible. Am I making any sense Mr. Harmon"?

"You are making a lot of sense, but did you convince our audience"?

Up to this point, the audience had been held captive and silent when all at once, they gave Erika a standing ovation! The clapping and the cheering went on for a full minute. There was no doubt in Erika's mind or in J. D's and Danelle's mind for that matter, that their fans believed her angelic message.

J.D. addressed the audience by saying; "Doesn't it make you feel good knowing that we have heavenly guardians looking out for us, even if we can't see them? One day, maybe we'll be granted the privilege of being able to see our Guardian Angels, whom some call 'Beings of Light' while others call them 'Spirit Guides'. It makes no difference whatsoever what you call them, as long as you don't ignore them. The bottom line is this; Erika has been able to do this all her life and thought everyone else could do the same. She didn't realize until she was older that she had to be careful who she told or there would be consequences to pay. So, she kept silent except for her close circle of family and friends until last fall, when she had enough money saved to fly from Whitehorse to Saint John, NB to attend one of our Psychic Shows. Following our frequent phone conversations, she now feels confident that she is a normal human being with special insights. Is this correct, Erika"?

Taking the microphone from J.D., Erika answered, "Yes it is, Mr. Harmon. May I say something to the audience?"

"Go ahead Erika," he replied. Turning to the audience, she continued; "Attending the J. D. Harmon Show has really made a huge difference in my life. I grew up as a very unhappy child because the ones closest to me thought I was acting strange. I remember being 'caught' talking to myself by one of my babysitters and running to my room crying after she told me that it wasn't nice to do what I was doing, that only really old people who were senile talked to themselves and that I should stop".

"Once in my room, my very own Guardian Angel, whose name is Mika, consoled me and helped me understand that I was different from other children that one day humanity would understand. And see, it's happening, thanks to Mr. Harmon and his wife. They've become great and valued friends." She passed the microphone back to J. D.

"We value your friendship also Erika yourself! Thank you for sharing your story with our viewers," after which Erika was escorted back to her seat. J.D. continued, "Now, I'd like to present to you, Mr. Connor Harrigan. This young man, with the help of someone like myself, is able to foregress or presage into the future." More applause from the audience as they recognized him from previous presentations.

"Connor has the special gift of spontaneous transportation, but he hasn't yet mastered the ability to control his mind. How have you been keeping Connor; Any more unwanted trips?"

"Hardly any Mr. Harmon, thanks to you. Now that you've showed me how to control my 'urge' to travel, I am nowhere the nervous person I used to be".

"That's great news Connor. Now, about being so nervous, are you referring to the time you travelled to the moon and back and thought you were losing your mind? You even made an unscheduled appointment with a psychiatrist, didn't you"?

"That's exactly right, Mr. Harmon. I went to see Dr. O'Brien".

"Was Dr. O'Brien able to help you understand what was happening"?

"No Mr. Harmon, he told me that against his better judgment, he was sending me to see his friend, you!" At that comment, the audience responded by standing up and clapping.

"Now Connor, how did "I" help you understand what was happening to you?"

"You told me that when my 'mind' and my 'will' merge together, I am able to experience a phenomenon called presaging, also known as time travelling".

"Right on, Connor! Keep up the good work. Can you give us an example of at least one other person who was able to do the same"?

"He was known as "Le Cure d'Ars, a priest living in a small village in France. His name was John Vianney. During his ministry, whether he was needed next door or on the other side of the continent, he found himself there in the blink of an eye and attributed all spontaneous transportation as the will of God. He was one of the holiest persons who lived in that century. He never abused the power handed to him but rather, he used it to help people in need".

"You remembered correctly Connor." Speaking to the audience, he continued; "If I may, I'll fill in a few blanks concerning Le Cure d'Ars. John Vianney, was born in 1786 in Dardilly, France and died in 1859 at the age of 73. In 1925, he was canonized a saint after living a life of service to his fellow man. Is there anything else you'd like to say to the audience Connor"?

"I've learned to curb my travelling fantasies. I've also learned that wishes cannot always be realized or when they do, it doesn't always make a person happy. It's also nice to keep your feet planted firmly on the ground," a statement that brought laughter from the audience.

"Thank you Connor." Connor Harrigan was then escorted to his seat amid an applauding crowd of grateful fans. Once more, J.D. has satisfied their curiosity and longing for the unknown.

A few seconds later, J. D. introduced his next guest to his eager audience.

"My dear people, here is another young man whom I greatly admire. His name is Jeremy Melvin. Jeremy has the ability to transport himself in time like Connor but without the help of anyone. Unlike Connor, who needs someone to guide him along his journeys, Jeremy can totally control his urge to 'time travel' on his own. You could say that he has mastered his special gift at an early age, bringing me to conclude that Connor will one day be able to do the same".

Jeremy has already volunteered to help Connor who, by the way, have become good friends. Now Jeremy, is there anything you want to convey to our audience tonight"?

"Yes Mr. Harmon, there is. For anyone who may be like Connor and I, this is what I want to say to you ; Accept your ability as a gift and not a curse. Along with all the other gifts God gave us, time travel must be used responsibly, with others best interest in mind.' "After which J. D. added, "In the next generations, we will hear more and more often of this phenomena. This is just the beginning of a period of time unknown to humankind. Our 'time out' may soon be coming to an end! When I say soon, this could mean hundreds of years seeing how long it has already been. Wouldn't that be marvelous"?

"Yeah!" came the cheering response from the audience.

J.D. continued, "I believe the Kingdom of God is now within our reach. Our privileges are about to be returned to us. Our 'time out' for having been disobedient is about to be restored and I can only speculate on what that will mean for humanity as a whole when that time arrives".

By the sound of the applause, Joel dared to hope that his purpose in life was being accomplished. He thanked Jeremy Melvin for appearing on tonight's show before he too was escorted to his seat.

It was time for another commercial break. The sweat was pouring from his forehead but Joel didn't mind. He felt as if he had accomplished something tonight that he'd never been able to accomplish previously. He couldn't begin to imagine how many people were tuned in to this special show. Taking hold of Danelle's hand, he invited his fans to stretch their legs for a few minutes, during the break.

*****

When he and Danelle returned on stage, each was holding a young girl by the hand, girls who looked amazingly alike. "Ladies and gentlemen, here are two sisters whom we met about six months ago. Please welcome the Donovan twins, Emily and Monica".

Both girls started waving as J. D. went on, "Like little Mohad, whom we talked about at the beginning of the show, Monica and Emily are able to communicate with animals, including birds and large insects such as butterflies and bumble bees. How have you been doing girls"?

"Great!" they answered in chorus. Emily seemed to have come out of her shy stage and was smiling at J.D. and Danelle. The girls had been so thrilled to learn they were going to personally meet Jeremy Melvin, Erika Latimer and Connor Harrigan. They had only heard of them by reading newspaper articles and in their innocent eyes, they were celebrities!

"How are all the animals doing girls?" Emily answered first looking at Monica for support.

"They're glad that spring is here. Some of them had a hard time during the winter months." Monica took over, saying, "Especially the cats and dogs. Some of their owners forget to let them in on cold nights while others leave them to find their own food and food is very scarce in winter".

"The birds though," said Emily, "are very happy. They never complain and they sing a lot, especially when they find bird seeds. The red cardinals are especially nice birds. Last summer, the hummingbirds were really grateful for the liquid nectar and the sugared water people left for them in those pretty red bottles. They told us they rely on nectar to gain enough energy to fly south for the winter. They are so smart! The woodpeckers are much harder to understand and have only one thing on their mind, making noise!"That made the audience chuckle.

"The rabbits and the deer find it extremely hard to find food on the snow covered ground. The squirrels and chipmunks aren't so bad, because they get ready for winter in the fall. The raccoons are always busy and told me that the days are not long enough".

"Well girls, I can't tell you how nice it is to hear from the animals," J. D. said. "Is there anything else you'd like to say, maybe something important to someone out there"?

"Yes! We want to say hello to someone who lives far away in Brazil, someone named Mohad who is just like us. Maybe we can meet you someday Mohad. Hope you're listening!"

"Yes, I hope he's listening too. Is there anything else you would like to say?"

"Yes there is Mr. Harmon. The Monarch butterflies are worried that they won't have a place to migrate in the winter months. They told us that they are guided by celestial information which regulates their biological clock. When they arrived in Mexico last winter, after flying 2000 miles, the Mexican people rejoiced and celebrated their arrival but then, it was discovered that half of the tall trees in which they cling to for months had been cut down and there wasn't enough trees left for the monarchs to stay for the usual period of five months. They had to fly north again and a lot of them perished".

"We are so sorry to hear that!" A big sigh was heard throughout the theatre. "Thank you so much girls, for sharing with us your knowledge of the animals and the insects. I hope no more trees will be destroyed so the monarch butterflies will have a resting place this coming fall. You may now join your Mom and Dad".

Addressing his audience, he stated; "Extraordinary things can be accomplished by ordinary people". Looking right at the cameras, J. D. asked: "How many of you out there wish you could go public with your knowledge without being made to feel like an outcast or made fun of? If you're watching this program, we would love to hear from you".

J. D. then went on to give his address and phone number, adding, "Danelle and I would be honoured to meet with you." Turning back to his audience, he continued; "After the next commercial, we'll do a demonstration with each of the other special guests. Thank you for your interest". It had been an interesting evening so far and the audience was expecting even more.

Chapter 15

A few days following the televised J. D. Harmon Show, the phone began to ring almost non-stop. A lot of these calls were legitimate while others weren't. The Harmons were at loose end to determine which ones of those callers were really telling the truth.

One call came from a young woman by the name of Jordyn Chamberlain.

Joel, who happened to take that particular call, was intrigued when she told him that she was able to find water using only a wooden stick, called a dowsing rod.

Joel knew that this theory was proven to be true, but

he had never met anyone with this specific talent called 'divining'. The wooden stick used by the diviner, also called a dowser, is made in the shape of a wishbone and when held in front of the dowser, it begins to sway on it's own, even indicating how deep the water is underground by an upward and a downward pull. This method has been used effectively for centuries, helping people who needed to dig a well. In this day and age, it is still considered an effective means of finding water for individuals planning to drill a well. It saves a lot of time and money. The only problem is to find a good dowser. Although this gift is a fairly common occurrence, no one is sure if it is inherited or if it comes about by other means. In this instance, it seems to have come down through the family tree. One of Jordyn's aunt supposedly possessed the same talent. So, Joel made an appointment to meet with Jordyn Chamberlain. If all worked out well, she would be appearing on the next J. D. Harmon show. This would make an interesting change and even Joel was curious to see how dowsing worked.

Another phone call proved to be very interesting. This time, Danelle took the call and later relayed the information to Joel. Apparently, this older lady had the gift of touch healing. All through her life, she'd been called to the sickbed of dozens of people who, miraculously had been healed of their ailments, healings that had left family members and the medical institution baffled. As Joel was taking notes, he asked Danelle for the lady's name. Her name was Tina Stevenson and a descendant of the Loyalists. They agreed to meet her for a demonstration.

The Harmons came to realized that the gift of healing was far more common than first thought, for the next call was also from a woman, this time of French Acadian decent. Her name was Lisa d'Entremont, who claimed to have healing hands. The energy to heal came from the palm of her hands in the form of heat. She was a Reiki Master, an ancient custom used in healing without ever touching the body. She went on to explain to Danelle that warm energy could be felt emitting from her hands or, for that matter any Reiki master's hands, but it required meditation and concentration. Danelle was impressed and so was Joel. They arranged to meet with her also.

Half a dozen e-mail messages confirmed that this gift of healing was by far the most common. A couple of brothers claimed to be able to heal themselves. Terry and Gary Mulligan would be interviewed in person as it was impossible to come to a decision by reading their e-mail. By the end of the week, Joel and Danelle had found quite an assortment of people claiming to be gifted. Now, the sifting through would begin.

"It's a good thing we only had one televised show," Danelle told Joel. "Isn't it great though, to see how far the human race has evolved, especially in the last century. What do you think we'll see happening next Joel"?

"My greatest desire, as well as for most people I'm sure, would be to experience global peace. I also realize that this could take a lot longer than my lifespan. Hopefully, our grandchildren will live to witness it". She looked at him with a twinkle in her eyes.

"Did I hear you mention grandchildren Joel dear? Shouldn't there be children first before even considering having grandchildren? You're making me feel ancient honey".

"Sweets, if you want to get a head start with the children, just say the word".

"Oh yea? It might be sooner than you think".

"What do you mean, sooner than I think"?

"How about in just over seven months"?

"What! Danelle, are you pregnant? Are you telling me that we're having a baby"? Danelle broke into hysterical laughter seeing the expression on his face.

"We are, aren't we? My God, I'm going to be a daddy!" He picked her up and twirled her around the room. "How long have you known sweets"?

"I've only found out this afternoon. I've been trying to come up with a spectacular way of telling you, but I couldn't pass up your grandchildren comment. I'm so excited Joel! Do you think we'll be good parents"? she asked with concern in her voice.

"I'm sure we will be, although I've never been a parent before. Do we need to take a course or something? When are we going to tell our families? I can't wait to tell Frisco".

"To answer your first question, no we don't have to take a course. Being a parent comes naturally. Mom will be so thrilled! She hinted about it last time we visited.

She informed me she would like to become a grandmother before she was too old to enjoy it. I had to remind her that she and Dad are only in their fifties. Also, that we'd only been married for three months. Joel, I honestly think we got pregnant on the last leg of our honeymoon".

"Great timing, wouldn't you say?" he replied. They giggled like a pair of teenagers. The Harmons were among the happiest couple alive!

Expecting a baby seems to have that effect on young married couples. They carried on the rest of the day, making plans that would include a third person in their new family. They decided to wait a few more weeks before telling relatives. It was all so exuberating!

CHAPTER 16

The interviews began shortly after the last phone calls were screened. It wasn't an easy job. Joel and Danelle had been advised by Tom to be very careful as it only took one bad apple to ruin the whole barrelful. By following his advice, it proved to be a long process. Meanwhile, Danelle was getting use to being an expectant mother. She found the mornings hard to deal with, loosing quite a few breakfasts, but she knew it would be all worth it the day she would be able to hold her precious baby in her arms. Drunk with happiness, she anticipated becoming a new mom with gusto.

After two weeks, they couldn't keep it a secret any longer. They paid Kelsey and Frisco a visit first. It proved to be a welcoming piece of information for the O'Briens. Their children were still young enough to be able to play with their cousin. That same night, they called Danelle's mom and dad. Her mom was ecstatic knowing she was finally going to become a grandmother before the year was over; as were Joel's parents when they received the call. Edith ran over next door to give Gabrielle the happy news. They were like one big, happy family!

A month later, Kelsey was already planning a baby shower, but Danelle asked her to hold off until at least the middle of July. Their next show was scheduled for July 8th, so she knew that between planning this event and working, she'd be too busy to enjoy a baby shower.

One by one, they met with the people who would be considered for future guests on their upcoming shows. The first one to be interviewed was Jordyn Chamberlain. As a precaution, Joel asked for I. D. to confirm her identity. She had been advised on the phone that she would be required to demonstrate her ability to dowse. So, she showed up at the Harmon's with her dowsing rod. As the demonstration would be most effective outside, she asked them to accompany her to the back yard. She led them as far as the fence enclosing their property, all the while explaining the procedure to both Joel and Danelle. That's when the divining rod seemed to acquire a life of its own. Jordyn, holding the forked branch, started walking backward. First, the branch began to sway from left to right and then, started going up and down. Joel tried to steady it with his hand, but found it impossible. There was definitely a strong gravity pull coming from somewhere under their feet.

"My guess," Joel said to Jordyn "is that there must be water close by, am I correct"?

Danelle was spell bound. She had never seen anything like that!

Jordyn confidently answered, "Yes, Mr. Harmon, there

is. Let me move forward a bit and we can start counting the depth in feet where water can be found".

The movement of the rod seemed to go on forever when abruptly, it stopped. Jordyn looked at J. D. and smiled. "Mr. Harmon, if you wanted to dig for water right here on this spot, you'd have to go down 110 feet, give or take a few feet."

"Honestly? That's incredible"! Both he and Danelle were very impressed, to say the least. They couldn't wait to have Jordyn appear on their next show. Their fans were sure to welcome something new.

That evening, they were still talking about Jordyn Chamberlain when Danelle mentioned her upcoming interview with Lisa d'Entremont. Joel reminded her he had another commitment and wouldn't be home until quite late. Would she mind doing the interview by herself?

Danelle wasn't sure how she would conduct the interview with Miss d'Entremont. She couldn't expect to witness a healing because no one was sick. But Joel assured her that she'd know and not to worry about it. So she went about her chores and Joel left for his appointment.

Right on time, the doorbell rang and Danelle found herself looking at an attractive woman in her early 40's. She instantly felt at ease with this woman who spoke in a very gentle voice. Lisa's eyes brightened as she noticed Danelle's 'condition' which was just beginning to show; "You're expecting a baby! How exciting!"

"Nice to meet you, Miss d'Entremont. And yes, it is a great feeling to know a little baby is growing bigger every day that goes by," Danelle said, patting her tummy. "Make yourself comfortable Miss d'Entremont."

"Please call me Lisa. I gather all is going well with your pregnancy"?

"My doctor tells me everything is normal and that I'm carrying a healthy baby. So Lisa, how do you plan on convincing me that you have the gift of healing"?

"First," replied Lisa, "I'll show you my credentials." She drew a long sheet of paper from her purse.

"This," she said, "is my Reiki Master's certificate. "I'll try to explain as much as possible about this healing process called Reiki. Are we ready"?

"I'm ready and also quite anxious to hear about it so, go right ahead" Danelle told her as she led the way to the living room.

"Thank you. The healing comes from laying hands 'over' the afflicted area of the body and asking the Creator God to give me the energy needed to heal that part of the body of it's ailment".

"Interesting, indeed!"

"The energy emitted from the palms of my hands is not of my own doing, but comes from a higher source of power, being the Spirit of God. Are you a believer, Mrs. Harmon"?

"Yes, I am and please, no formal names, call me Danelle".

"Then, call me Lisa, please" as she continued; "This kind of healing is done without ever touching the ailing part of a person's body. I could demonstrate that part to you. Don't be alarmed if you feel heat coming from my hands. I have a feeling your back is bothering you today, am I right?"

"As a matter of fact, it is. How could you tell"?

"I'm able to 'see' pain, if you can understand what that means. 'Auras' are manifested around every living person, some auras being more pronounced than others, depending on their spiritual advancement. Yours is very pronounced I must say".

"Very interesting, Lisa. Please continue".

"Where there is pain, the color of the aura changes, from blue to pink to red. The aura around your lower back is now pink, meaning that you are experiencing discomfort but certainly not deep pain. If you don't mind standing up, I'll demonstrate something to you".

"Not at all," Danelle said as she promptly got up from the couch.

Lisa began to rub her hands together and asked Danelle

to turn around. She then placed the palm of her hands about an inch away from Danelle's lower spine area and Danelle could only blink back in surprise. It felt as if the hot rays of the sun were shining on her back. A feeling of well-being enveloped her lower back while the heat seemed to seep through her whole body. She turned around to make sure Lisa wasn't holding a lit candle or any other gadget that would have provided the heat she was experiencing, but Lisa had her eyes closed in concentration. Danelle didn't say a word; she just enjoyed the feeling of well being that was enveloping her lower back. When Lisa finally spoke, Danelle turned around and she witnessed the look of wonder on Danelle's face.

"You felt it, didn't you"?

"I sure did. That was incredible! My back feels totally relaxed. I'm not sure how you did it but thank you Lisa".

"You're welcome. Do you think I qualify to appear on the famous J. D. Harmon Show"?

"I think you just passed the test Lisa".

"Thank you, Danelle. I hope your pregnancy goes well to the end".

"We'll be in touch to tell you when to expect to appear on one of our shows". 'This Reiki business is something else' Danelle said to herself as she closed the door behind Lisa d'Entremont. She couldn't wait to tell Joel about it! The fans would love to hear what Lisa had to say.

CHAPTER 17

All across the country, people began to show interest in the J.D. Harmon Show. One of these people was a person by the name of Ron Carpenter, claiming he was a well known tea leaf reader. Danelle had never heard of such a thing as tea leaf reading, but Joel said he remembered seeing an article about it in a magazine. Mr. Carpenter asked the Harmons if they would be interested in meeting with him for a demonstration of his tea-leaf reading ability.

"We'll call you after we've had a chance to discuss it, how is that"?

After consulting with each other, Danelle said, "I think we should give him a chance, don't you?"

"I suppose we'll never know for sure if we don't interview him and see what he can accomplish with tea leaves".

So, Danelle called him back; arranged an appointment for a meeting and before they hung up Mr. Carpenter asked her if she could purchase a package of loose tea before their meeting. She said she would. Oh boy, she would never have thought of that! But it sure made a lot of sense. They always used tea bags for their cup of tea and even though she didn't know anything about tea leaf reading, she asked Joel "how could this Mr. Carpenter read a tea bag?" She laughed out loud. She had such a happy disposition lately that Joel commented on it.

"If it makes you this happy to be expecting a baby, I think I'll keep you pregnant year after year" he joked.

"Joel honey, tell me those same words after you've

stayed up three nights in a row with a colicky baby, then I'll believe you".

"You mean this could actually happen? You know how I hate losing my sleep. I'll be as grouchy as a bear," Joel exaggerated.

"Then, I'll have to tame you, won't I?" Danelle replied, laughing.

Ron Carpenter showed up bright and early the following Monday morning. He was a jolly man with grey, fuzzy hair and a white beard, probably in his late sixties.

"Come in, Mr. Carpenter. My husband is presently on the phone in the study, but he will be out shortly. Can I get you a cold drink or would you prefer something hot maybe, like tea?" she said, winking to him.

"Don't mind if I do, Mrs. Harmon", he replied, his crinkled eyes full of life. "Tea is my favourite. Which one of you is the tea drinker?"

"As a matter of fact, both of us are and we can't wait to see a demonstration of tea leaves reading".

"My fingers are itching to show you," he replied

Joel walked into the room, introducing himself. "Nice to meet you Mr. Carpenter, I'm Joel Harmon and I see you've already met my wife Danelle. Sorry if I've kept you waiting".

"No problem, I was having a nice little chat with your wife. Call me Ron, everyone else does."

"O. K. Ron, how do we begin"?

"First" he chuckled, "you have to be a good boy and drink all your tea. Then we will see what's in store for you and the Mrs."

"Oh, and did the Mrs brew a pot of tea?" Joel asked, mischief in his voice.

"I did," she answered, "I'll go and pour each of us a cup".

Over the half hour that it took for the three of them to sip their tea, Ron Carpenter informed the Harmons that his gift of tea leaf reading had been taught to him by an old Indian Chief.

"That old Indian was 'at one' with the universe. He once performed a rain dance and by golly, it worked. If I hadn't been there to witness it with my own eyes, I don't think I would have believed it. This goes to show how powerful the mind is when it's in tune with the universe. Of course, I may be old and stupid, but I believe that the mind of God 'is' the universe. Do you believe there is a God overlooking the whole thing Mr. Harmon?" he asked, swirling his hand around, indicating the horizon.

"You bet I do! How else could we explain life? To this day, there is so much that remains a mystery where life is concerned, isn't there"?

"I agree with you one hundred percent Mr. Harmon. My brother Don is a medical Doctor and used to be very skeptical when I talked to him about the supernatural. Much too long of a story to get into at the moment, suffice to say that he has had a change of heart".

"I think I understand what you mean. Some people

need to have proof or else they think you're trying to fill their head with nonsense," Danelle replied.

"You've got it right on the dot, Mrs. Harmon".

"I gather you're now retired Mr. Carpenter?" Joel asked him.

"That, I am. Best decision I ever made".

"Do you mind my asking what profession you retired from?" Joel asked him.

"I was a policeman. Very fulfilling job, although it could be a little hair raising at times".

"I'm sure it was, but remember that the world is a much better place because of people like you," Danelle told him.

"Thank you, young lady".

Joel spoke next. "Are we ready to begin? My cup is empty, how about yours Danelle"?

"Yes, I'm all done".

"Very well, you can turn your cups upside down in the

saucer to make sure every last drop of liquid is drained. Which one of you do you want me to read first"?

Joel graciously tipped his head toward Danelle and said, "ladies first."

Ron Carpenter gently picked up Danelle's cup, giving it his full attention. When he finally looked up at her, he pointed inside the cup and her breath caught and her eyes opened wide as she saw what he was pointing at. A tiny cradle!

"I'm not blind, so it's no secret that you're expecting a baby, but for you to see this formation inside your cup seems to have taken you by surprise," Ron Carpenter said. Joel was stretching his neck to be able to take a peek inside the cup too. Then he saw it and gasped.

"Now, look over the cradle, yes right there", Mr. Carpenter said, pointing at something, close to the top of the cup.

"That looks like a 'G'!" Danelle exclaimed.

"Yes, it does. What do you suppose it could mean?"

Ron Carpenter asked with a grin on his weather beaten face.

"A Girl? Am I having a girl"?

"Yep, that seems to be the case. You're having a girl, no doubt about it".

Joel brought his arm around Danelle's bulging waist. "We're having a girl! We're having a girl!" He was just about jumping for joy.

"Now, your cup Mr. Harmon." Joel handed him his cup. After a thorough examination, he exclaimed, "Ah! Let me see, what is this, on the right side of your cup?"

"Where do you mean, right here? It looks like the shape of an airplane. What do you suppose it means Mr. Carpenter? We don't plan on taking any more trips for quite some time".

"Call me Ron. What else do you see on the bottom of your cup, close to the airplane"?

"Now, let's see, it looks like a pair of B's. A small one and a large one".

"Exactly! Those B's have to be associated with the airplane. Is there a possibility that someone could be flying to see you, let's say from a place associated with the letter 'B'? "

All of a sudden, it dawned on Joel, his thought being instantly transferred to Danelle.

"My God! Danelle, could it be that little boy in Brazil is coming to see us? Could someone in his family have seen our show on T.V. and somehow relayed our message to Mohad's mother"?

"Brazil, you say? Why so far?" Ron asked. He was at a loss to figure out what these two were talking about.

Seeing the confused look on Ron Carpenter's face, Joel went on to explain.

"We were visiting Rio de Janeiro on our honeymoon and wondered away to a small village where we met a little boy named Mohad who was very special. He was hiding behind a tree as if he had done something wrong. We tried to talk to him but he wouldn't answer. His mother came along and pulled him against her as if he needed to be protected from us. It was hard to communicate with them as their English was very limited, especially the mother. Finally, the little boy said a few words to us in English, and then translated it to the woman whom we assumed was his mother. Thankfully, after a few minutes of very slow communication, a man showed up and explained to us what the mother was trying to say. We were hoping against all odds, to be able to meet that little boy again one day, especially following our televised show last month. Is it a possibility, do you think"?

"Definitely a possibility, but I don't make any promises, ever. I don't want to give people false hope. What was it that the mother was trying to tell you, if you don't mind my asking"?

"She was telling us that her son was 'troubled' because he liked to talk with animals" Joel told Ron. "But if they or someone they knew saw our televised show, they might have heard the Donovan twins pleading with Mohad and relayed their message", Joel stated, daring to hope that was the case.

"Time will tell," Ron Carpenter answered, patting the top of his head. "Didn't I have a cap on my head when I came in? I'm always losing my cap, no matter where I go".

Danelle was still dazed by the possibility of little Mohad coming for a visit, her eyes saying much more than her lips.

Joel, looking around the room answered, "I don't know Ron, I wasn't in this room when you first came in. Did you notice a hat laying around, Danelle dear"?

Danelle came out of her reverie long enough to realize what Mr. Carpenter was looking for. "Ah, I'm so sorry Mr. Carpenter, I mean Ron. My mind was roaming. Your cap is right over there, on the buffet beside the door". Ron Carpenter got up and both Joel and Danelle accompanied him to the door.

"I'll be waiting to hear from you. Now tell me, what did you think of my reading? Did I make an impression"?

"A big impression, if you must know" Danelle replied.

"Gee, thanks," Ron replied, a big grin on his bearded face.

"You'll be contacted as soon as we have a date for you to come and demonstrate your amazing skill," Joel told him while shaking his hand. "Take care Mr. Carpenter and God bless".

"It's Ron, and God bless you too"!

After he had gone, Joel looked at Danelle and exclaimed, "Wow! That was a lot of information from two cups of tea".

"You can say that again. But Joel, listen to this. Isn't tea leaf reading also a sort of presaging? Assuming any of these predictions were to come true, that is".

"It is, now that you mention it. Presaging means anything from the future that is projected to the present time. And that is what he did really, by predicting events that have yet to take place".

"Oh Joel, I hope he was right; at least the part about the boy from Brazil. As far as us having a little girl, sure I'd love having a little girl but I would also love having a little boy just as much. It makes no difference to me what we have. All I want is our precious baby, yours and mine".

"I'm with you on that one".

"Let's go find something to eat, I'm starving. I haven't eaten anything in two full hours"!

CHAPTER 18

While watching a program on television one evening, Danelle's attention was captured upon hearing about a little girl whom they referred to as an 'indigo child'. She became really interested in the program and called Joel to come and see what was on. Upon hearing the interview with the parents of the child, Joel told Danelle that he would love to speak with that little girl. Apparently, this incredible little five year old girl left her parents dumfounded with the knowledge she displayed on many occasions. When her father was asked what it was that his daughter could do that made her so unusual, he replied that listing what she 'couldn't' do would be a lot easier. He then gave a few examples as to what he meant by that statement.

At the age of three, their daughter Josie had shown interest in violin music. Every time she saw someone on T.V. playing the violin, she clapped her hands and watched intently until it was over. One day, her father asked her if she would like to play one of those instruments and her response was "yes daddy, I would love to play the violin." At that point, he didn't even think she had that word in her vocabulary.

The very next day, he and his wife brought Josie to a music shop. To the amazement of the shop owner, she pointed to a violin saying, "Could I please try this violin sir?"

Looking at Josie's parents he said: "You mean to tell me that this child can play this instrument? How old is she anyway?"

"She'll be four in three months" her mother replied, "and we don't know that she can play because this will be the first time she touches a violin. We're just as anxious to find out as you are".

The violin was taken down from the shelf on the wall and passed on to Josie. With a doubtful look on his face, the store owner motioned for her to go ahead and try it, hoping she wouldn't drop and smash it. Josie looked at it for a moment, turned it around to look at the back, and then examined the strings and the 'archet'. She then went on to fit it under her chin and began to play a popular melody. It was awesome to hear this young child produce such heavenly music! And this was without ever having taken music lessons! The three of them stood frozen into place, hardly able to believe their ears!

When she was done, Josie handed the violin and the bow back to the store owner and started clapping her hands the way she had done at home watching the violinist on television.

"We didn't know you could play the violin honey. How

did you learn to do that?" her mother asked, moved to tears.

"Oh mommy, I watched the man on T. V. and then I remembered how to play".

The store owner didn't know what to believe but he couldn't deny what he had just heard with his own ears. "What else can your child do? I suppose you're going to tell me she can sing like a bird, and I would certainly believe you after what I've just heard. What's your name little girl?" he asked, shaking his head to make sure he wasn't dreaming.

"Josie. I'm Josie Quinlan, sir," she answered, extending her small hand toward him.

"Well Josie, I'm very honoured to meet such a talented young musician. I hope to see you again". That's when he turned around to shake hands with us and declared, "Your daughter is an amazing child who will make it big in the music world. Take good care of her".

"That was the first time we realized Josie was gifted with musical talent" the father was saying to the interviewer at the end of the program.

Danelle turned the T. V. off and looked at Joel. "Well, what do you think honey?"

"I'm speechless, that's what I think. Did you ever hear anything like it"?

"I can't say that I have. Could she be the reincarnation of a famous musician? At the beginning of the program, she was referred to as an 'indigo child'. I've never heard that term spoken before, how about you"?

"No never, but it might be worth investigating. I'm sorry to disagree with you sweets, but I don't believe in reincarnation. I believe our souls, the souls of all human beings, were created at the same time, on the day of creation. Then God gives us the choice to live on earth by depositing our soul in a human body as it is conceived. This is what I mean by 'returning to the source of our greater joy' at the moment of death. We finally return to the place where we were first created".

"I'm just realizing now that there is still a great deal to learn about you Joel. Now, I want to find out more about 'indigo children'. Let's go on the internet and see what we can come up with".

After an hour of searching every website that could provide them with any sort of information on 'indigo children' Joel and Danelle were satisfied with the knowledge that this little Josie was indeed what was referred to as an 'indigo child.' There was a wealth of information on the websites, enough that it had piqued their curiosity. They knew that they would do everything in their power to meet with Josie Quinlan and her parents. Tom would know how to get hold of Global Television which had hosted the program. They were both very excited when they went to bed that night.

The following day, Joel was waiting in his office to hear what Tom had been able to find out about Josie Quinlan.

"What were you able to come up with my friend?" he asked Tom.

"Not very much I'm afraid. It seems the parents are very protective of their daughter, making sure no one tries to exploit her. And you can't really blame them".

"I agree with you wholeheartedly," Joel replied. "But please keep trying, something may come up."

It turned out to be the Quinlans who got in touch with the Harmons. Carl and Annette Quinlan, Josie's parents had been assured by the television station that their address and phone number would be kept confidential after their T.V. interview. Tom must have been very convincing because Global had contacted the Quinlans and told them about J.D. Harmon's inquiries. Even though they lived in another province, Annette and Carl knew about the famous clairvoyant and didn't see any harm in talking to him. Plus, Josie wanted to talk to the famous physic that she had once watched on television. She had become very entranced with those who had appeared as special guests, especially so when J. D. had interviewed the incredible twins. Her mom recalled the event, for Josie had not wanted to leave the T.V. room until the show was over.

On Monday morning, the phone rang at the Harmon's house as Joel and Danelle were ready to leave for work. "Harmon's residence, good morning," Joel said as he picked up the telephone.

"Good day Mr. Harmon. My name is Carl Quinlan and I was told that you are interested in meeting our little girl?"

"You bet I am Mr. Quinlan. Where are you calling from"?

"We live in Stratford, Ontario".

"This is a nice surprise sir. My wife and I have watched part of the interview with your daughter and we found her to be extremely fascinating! Would it be possible to meet with you and your wife and of course with Josie"?

There was a period of silence before he responded. "First I must tell you that my wife and I are very concerned for our daughter's well being and will go to any length to keep her from being hurt in any way or by anyone. I want to make this clear to you Mr. Harmon".

"For starters, let me assure you that I would never hurt a child, mentally or otherwise. My wife and I are expecting our first child and I already feel protective toward our baby, so I understand your concern sir. I wouldn't want my child to be exploited for someone else's gain. You have nothing to fear from us Mr. Quinlan".

"Then tell me Mr. Harmon, what is the purpose of wanting to meet our daughter?"

"Because Mr. Quinlan, I'm convinced that your daughter was born on this earth to accomplish great things. Does Josie know who I am"?

"Yes she does and she also wants to meet with you. How about that!"

"Is she standing there beside you?"

"As a matter she is".

"I knew it! My God, even from this far away, she's able

to communicate with me telepathically. That's incredible! When can we schedule an appointment for a meeting? That is, if you want, I don't want to pressure you. Either you come here or we go there, which ever you decide." Turning to Danelle, he exclaimed, "She wants to meet us too".

On the other end of the phone, he heard Mr. Quinlan say, "Do you mind if my wife and I discuss this matter tonight and call you back in the morning?"

"Sure, we wouldn't want you to make a hasty decision".

"Considering the time difference, I don't want to call too early. Would nine o'clock our time be O. K. with you"?

"Perfect, we'll be waiting for your call," Joel replied.

"Sorry if I sounded a bit brusque with you Mr. Harmon. My wife and I only want what's best for our little girl".

"No problem whatsoever, Mr. Quinlan. I understand

completely. We'll talk tomorrow, goodbye and give our regards to Josie".

CHAPTER 19

The following morning, Joel was up at the crack of dawn for he was too worked up to sleep any longer. An hour later, he peeked into the bedroom to see if Danelle was awake but she was still sleeping like a baby, or so he thought. He looked at the clock. It wasn't yet seven o'clock, so there was still an hour left before the phone would ring.

"I'll let her sleep another half hour," Joel muttered to himself. After the phone call last night, he and Danelle had decided to do a conference call to make sure they got all the facts straight. He had just closed the bedroom door when he heard "Joel dear, what time is it?"

"Oh, it's only seven o'clock. Take your time, there's still an hour left before they call".

"My gosh Joel, why didn't you wake me up sooner? I'll be all groggy when they call".

"Sorry honey, I haven't been up that long myself".

"You haven't? Then why are you shaved and dressed and why do I smell toast all over the house? If I didn't know you like the back of my hand, I'd say you were anxious about something. Come here and give 'us' a hug so 'we' can get dressed too".

"Gladly but hurry, we wouldn't want to keep the phone ringing too long, would we? You never know, they might change their mind".

"Heaven forbid. No we wouldn't want that to happen"!

At precisely eight o'clock, nine Ontario time, the phone rang. Joel looked at Danelle and said, "This is it, pick up the extension. I just hope they haven't changed their mind." Picking up the phone he said "Good morning, you have reached the Harmon's residence."

"Good morning to you sir, I think you were expecting my call"?

"That we were Mr. Quinlan. My wife and I were anticipating your call and we're anxious to hear of your decision".

"Then I won't keep you in suspense any longer. The answer is yes, we will meet with you".

"That is great news! And what have you decided to do? Come here to New Brunswick or have us meet you in Stratford"?

"Either way Mr. Harmon, it's going to cost you the amount of two tickets, ours or yours, but if you're willing to pay for Josie's ticket as well as ours, we're willing to fly to New Brunswick." Joel just about shouted, "We'll pay for hers too. That's great! How about this coming weekend? Do you have any plans?"

"None that can't be changed. Just a second, I'll check with Annette, that's my wife".

It only took half a minute and he was back on the phone. "Yes, that would be perfect. Will you make the arrangements?"

"We sure will. An early flight will bring you here early Saturday afternoon. We'll pick you up at the airport. Thank you so much Mr. Quinlan. Danelle and I can't wait to meet Josie. Oh yes, your tickets will be waiting for you at the airport, but you should call and confirm the time of departure".

"Will do. Goodbye then and we're looking forward to meeting you also," he said before he hung up the phone. Danelle hadn't had the chance to say one word. So much for the conference call!

Flight reservations were made as soon as they hung up the phone. Joel and Danelle were busy the rest of that week looking up more information on 'indigo children'. By Saturday, they were like two kids on Christmas morning.

After breakfast, they called the airport to check the arrival time of their guests' flight and were told it would land in Saint John at eleven forty five.

On their way to the airport, the Harmons discussed where they could take their guests for lunch. Planning to include a child was new to them but at the end, they agreed on Swiss Chalet.

The plane arrived on time and as soon as the family of three appeared through the gate, the Harmons knew it had to be them. Danelle remembered somewhat from the interview on T.V. but it hadn't done justice to the sweet little girl who was walking toward them. She just pinpointed Joel and Danelle and no words were necessary. She was indeed a special child. She stood right in front of them and smiled, extending her small hand toward Joel and then toward Danelle. "Are you Mrs. Harmon?" she asked.

"Yes I am, and you must be Josie. It's so nice to finally

be able to meet you. Are these two grown- ups your Mom and Dad"?

"Yes, they are" she answered, running back to her parents. Carl Quinlan extended his hand and introduced his wife Annette.

"I see there's no need to introduce Josie. She seems to take an instant liking to both of you." Turning to Josie he said "Remember Josie, you can't just walk up to strangers and start talking. Just in case the strangers wouldn't be nice people like Mr. and Mrs. Harmon, O. K.?"

"Yes daddy, but I knew they wouldn't hurt me because their minds are just like mine. They talked to me before the words came out, didn't you Mr. Harmon"?

"Yes Josie, I did but your Dad is right. It is better not to talk to strangers, just in case".

"I know and I won't". She took hold of her mom's hand and said: "I'm really hungry mommy. Can we go eat? Maybe at Swiss Chalet?" she added timidly, looking at Danelle.

Her mom looked embarrassed but Danelle picked right up and announced that reservations had already been made at Swiss Chalet for lunch.

"What a coincidence," she added, winking at Josie.

"Goodie! I love going there! Are we going in your car"?

"Yes we are. You can even sit with us in the front, would you like that"?

"You mean right in the middle"?

"Exactly," said Joel , "but first, let's pick up your bags."

Josie was chatting away as if she'd always known the Harmons. Once in the car and on the way to the restaurant, she turned to Danelle and whispered, "are you going to have a baby Mrs. Harmon?"

"I am honey. What do you know about babies? Do they cry a lot? And how do you know when they're hungry"?

"Oh you'll know when she's hungry because she'll make a hungry sound".

"Did you say 'she'? How do you know she's a girl?" Danelle asked, looking at Joel to see if he had heard that comment.

"I just know she's a little girl like me. Are we almost there"?

"We're not far," Joel said "only a few more kilometers. I'm hungry too. A quarter chicken sounds really good at the moment. How about you"?

"Do I have to eat a quarter of a chicken? My stomach isn't very big," she said looking serious.

"We won't make her eat a quarter of a chicken, will we?" Joel asked, looking over his shoulder at the Quinlans sitting in the back seat.

"More like a wing" her parents replied.

"Yea! I love chicken wings".

"I think we've arrived," Danelle said, looking at this beautiful child sitting between her and Joel. She couldn't help putting her arm around her tiny shoulders. Josie's hair was golden blond and straight with a bang across her forehead. She had lively blue eyes and oh, so intelligent looking! When she glanced at her, she realized Josie knew exactly what she was thinking. It was a brand new experience for Danelle. During her whole life, Joel was the only one with whom she could communicate her thoughts telepathically. She was still deep in thoughts when she realized the car was at a standstill.

"Mrs. Harmon, we're here" Josie said, taking hold of Danelle's hand.

"No need to call me Mrs. Harmon, you can call me Danelle, O.K."?

Along with a beautiful smile, a bond was formed between the two.

That evening, as everyone was comfortably seated in the living room, Joel asked the Quinlans how they felt about letting Josie appear as a guest on the J. D. Harmon Show. Carl Quinlan replied that it depended on Josie, whether or not she would be comfortable to talk in front of an audience. Annette was more protective of her daughter.

Taking Josie's hand she said; "Where exactly will it leave her after the show is over? Will she be sought after by curious individuals? That's the only thing I'm worried about. I wouldn't want her to be hounded everywhere she went".

"I understand your concern Mrs. Quinlan. Is that what happened after the television interview, were you contacted or bothered in any way"?

"Well no, we weren't. I didn't think about that." Looking at Josie, she said "Honey, what do you think? Would it bother you to do an interview with Mr. and Mrs. Harmon in front of people"?

Josie let out a deep breath and said; "Mommy worries about me, but that is what mommies do, don't they Danelle? Will you worry about your little girl after she's born the way Mommy worries about me"?

"After meeting you doll, I'm positive that I will". Looking at Josie's mom, she added "But while you're here Mrs. Quinlan, you have absolutely nothing to worry about. I'll tell you what; we won't discuss this interview any more tonight. How about watching a good movie? We have tons of them. Joel will even make popcorn" she said, looking at a stunned Joel.

"Popcorn? You want me to make popcorn? Do we have those microwavable bags that say 'this side down"?

"Yes honey, those are the ones I mean. You can manage those, can't you? Unless you want Josie to show you how to lay the bag in the microwave." Josie was laughing really hard by this time.

"Daddy always asks Mom that question too. I don't think men are very good cooks," she said, giggling away. "Mommy and I always bake cookies and cakes, and they're good".

"Josie loves to cook and is actually quite good at it," replied her mother. "We will bake some cookies and send you some in the mail before Christmas. That is if you want some".

"We'd love to have some! Besides, I've never received

cookies in the mail. It'll be an experience. How will you send it, just by regular mail"?

"We'll send them by Priority Post to be sure they get to you the following day and still taste fresh".

"That will be great. By then, the baby will be a couple of months old. Do you suppose she'll want to taste one of your cookies Josie"?

"I don't think so Danelle," she giggled. "When is your baby going to arrive?"

"She is supposed to be born on or close to November 1st".

"I wish you could come with the baby and spend Christmas with us Danelle. Then it would be perfect, wouldn't it Mommy"?

"It would be perfect for us but I'm sure Mr. and Mrs. Harmon have families who would miss them if they spent Christmas with us".

"I suppose that's true" replied Josie, " but we'll be thinking about you".

"So will we, honey".

After breakfast the following morning, the Quinlans came to an agreement. They would remain in New Brunswick for an extra two days to be able to attend Tuesday night's show. It would save them a lot of travelling. Josie was coached by Joel and Danelle as to what questions she would be asked. She seemed very comfortable with the upcoming interview. All spent an enjoyable two days doing fun things, like going to the zoo on Monday morning. In the afternoon, they picked up Sebastian and Alexandra and went for ice cream, then to the park to do their favourite activity, fly kites. Josie was having a great time with her new friends. Even though she was only a few years older than Alexandra, she was like a mother hen around her and Sebastian. Frisco and Kelsey were astounded by this child's unusual grown up behavior.

On Tuesday evening, Josie looked like a little princess in her long pink dress. Her hair was done up in one braid falling just below her shoulders. Her mom had taken great care in getting her ready on time. J.D. and Danelle's fans were in for a treat that night.

Never had they seen a child so young talking and performing the way she did. Joel demonstrated to them how she could communicate with him and Danelle by telepathy. She was able to name all provinces and their capital cities as well as the name of all the planets. She was a walking encyclopedia! She had insisted on bringing her violin which she played beautifully for the audience. When Danelle asked her to tell the fans how she had learned to play so well, she replied that she had observed a violinist on television and learned from him. The members of the audience could only shake their heads in amazement!

Joel then asked Josie's parents to please come up and bring their daughter back to her seat, which they did but not before Josie bowed and waved to everyone. It was a memorable evening. She was the belle of the ball!

The Quinlan family left to go home the following

morning, but not before Josie asked Danelle to call them as soon as the baby was born.

"You'll be the first to know, I promise," Danelle whispered to Josie. She knew she would miss that little girl a lot! It was a good thing she only had to wait three more weeks for her own. She hugged Josie one more time and then it was time to board the plane. Joel and Danelle waved one more time before the Quinlans disappeared inside the jet.

"Come on Sweets, lets go home, you look tired," Joel told Danelle. She didn't answer, only reached for his hand as they went up the ramp, away from the lobby. One lone tear ran down her cheek. How could anyone be able to wrap themselves around your heart in such a short period of time? Danelle wondered. As she looked up, Joel answered her thought. "I know honey, I hated to see her leave too, but Ontario isn't on the other side of the globe. We'll go visit sometime soon or maybe they'll come back here. I don't like to see you so sad."

"I'll be O.K.. Let's go home and have something to eat, because I'm really hungry." As soon as they got inside the house, Joel fixed them each a sandwich and poured two glass of milk. After they had finished eating, Danelle looked up and said "I've been feeling a twinge across my back".

"A twinge? What kind of twinge? Not one like the doctor mentioned, is it? My Lord Danelle! You're not having the baby are you? There's still three weeks"!

"Well, not this minute I'm not. But I think it's getting close".

Seeing the look of horror on his face, she added; "I don't mean minute close but hour close, so don't panic O.K.? Let's get my suitcase and go. I'd rather be early so we don't have to rush". Joel ran to the bedroom and picked up a large case that was very light.

"Not that case Joel, the one I showed you the other day laying beside the closet door. I told you not to panic".

"I'm not panicking," he said, leading her outside to the driver's side of the car.

"Joel, I don't think it's a good idea for me to be driving".

"I'm driving, just give me time" Joel said, looking like a madman. Danelle burst out laughing. Her macho, sexy husband looked like a disheveled clown, running around the car.

"Joel dear, please calm down. There is no need to hurry, just put the suitcase in the backseat, relax and take me to the hospital. Does that sound reasonable to you honey?" At that very moment, a searing pain shot through her lower back. No more doubt, the baby was coming!

"Of course" Joel exclaimed "let's go"!

At 2 A.M. the morning of October 8, baby Arielle Elisabeth was born, exactly three weeks before her due date. In the eyes of her loving parents, she was perfect.

Being a new mom, the hospital kept Danelle and the baby until the next day. Joel was never too far from them.

He went out to eat and to sleep, then came right back to watch his infant daughter sleep, because that's all she seemed to be doing. He and Danelle marveled at their own little miracle of love laying in the hospital basinet.

Before lunch, as they were watching baby Arielle sleeping peacefully, Danelle asked Joel if he had remembered to call Josie's parents. He flipped open his cell and asked Danelle if she remembered their phone number.

"Only because it's such an unusual number. Here, I'll dial it".

It had only rang once when Josie answered. "Hi Danelle, I wanted to call but Mom wouldn't let me. The baby arrived didn't she"?

"I won't ask how you knew but yes Josie, Arielle Elisabeth arrived early this morning. She's quite a big girl at seven pounds, twelve ounces. As soon as we can, we'll send you photos by e-mail. How does that sound"?

"Great! She must be beautiful; I wish I could see her".

"You will honey, I promise. And yes, she is beautiful. How was your flight home"?

"It was good but I wish I was there".

"We'll plan to go for a visit soon. Joel says hello! I can't talk any more because cell phones shouldn't be used in a hospital. Don't forget to tell your Mom and Dad. Bye honey".

"I won't. Bye Danelle, bye Joel. I loved going to your house".

"We loved having you honey. Take care little princess. Goodbye"!

CHAPTER 20

It was Friday and time to bring Arielle home. Joel was up early and prepared the car with the new baby carrier that they had purchased only a couple of weeks previously.

Upon arriving at the hospital, he proudly announced to the receptionist at the front desk his reason for being there. Five minutes later, carrying the baby and holding Danelle's hand, the happy couple walked by the same desk.

"Congratulations, Mr. and Mrs. Harmon. It's always inspiring for me to see new parents go out those doors. It brings back memories of years ago".

"Thank you Mrs. Taylor and have a good day".

In the car, Danelle asked Joel if he had remembered to notify her work place because it had completely slipped her mind. "I told them last week to be prepared to replace me at a moment's notice. I just didn't think it would be this quick".

"I wouldn't have remembered, but there was a message on the phone when I got home yesterday. When you didn't show up at your regular time, they figured that you might have had the baby early. I did remember to call Kelsey though, and she promised to call the others. Mom and Dad were pretty excited too. How did your Mom react to the news"?

"Like any first time grandmother would I suppose. For lack of a better expression, she yelled like a cowboy rounding up a herd".

"I gather she was pleased it was a little girl?" Joel grinned.

"You bet she was! And so was Dad. I didn't know he

felt so strongly about becoming a grandfather. What about your parents? Do you think they would have preferred to have another grandson"?

"No, I didn't get that impression. They're already looking forward to a little brother for Arielle next year though".

"You're joking!" she said, her laughter echoing through the car.

*****

The next day, as Joel was planning his next performance which was still two weeks away, he asked Danelle how she felt about inviting Jordyn Chamberlain to come and explain to their audience what dowsing for water meant. Danelle thought it was a great idea, so Joel contacted Jordyn and she agreed to attend. The next show was scheduled for October 25th.

Kelsey was babysitting Arielle and Danelle had reluctantly parted with her darling little girl to attend the show. How did she exist before this precious infant was born? She would be content to just stay home and nurture her every minute of every day. It was love as only a mother can experience. But Joel had promised her they would come straight home as soon as the show was over, so she would try to enjoy herself. Besides, Arielle was in good hands, her aunt Kelsey was very pleased to baby-sit her. All the same, she would have rather stayed home.

"I hate to leave her, I love her so much" Danelle said to Joel.

"I love her too honey, but you know that Kelsey will take good care of her. It will do you good to be out with me tonight. You've been home for the past three weeks. Besides, the fans would miss not having you there. You've become part of the attraction you know. Now, if I didn't show up, probably nobody would notice" he joked.

"Thanks for trying to cheer me up. I'm simply suffering from 'new mom's blues' I guess".

An hour later, they were entering through the back door

of a large auditorium. Following the usual introductions, J.D. asked Tom to escort Jordyn Chamberlain on stage, something Tom was only too happy to do. He thought Jordyn was the most beautiful woman he ever saw. And by her blushing cheeks as he offered her his arm, she must have found him attractive too. Danelle and Joel didn't miss this interaction between the two.

"Jordyn, would you please explain to this audience what dowsing means because a lot of people have never heard of it".

Giving the audience her undivided attention, she began; "Dowsing, also called divining, is the ability to locate water underground using a method as old as history itself." Her next statement left even Joel taken aback.

"Dowsing isn't limited to finding water. It can also be used to locate precious metal, oil, precious stones or even landmines."

The 'ohs' and the 'ahs' from the audience prompted Joel

to interrupt her for a second. "Could you please describe to the audience what kind of object is used in dowsing"?

"Oh, sure. Centuries ago, the Egyptians used a forked stick, similar to what is being used today. Drawings of these objects have been found on excavated stone carvings or artifacts from that era. To this day, this is the most common tool used in dowsing". She bent down to retrieve something from her oversized bag. "Like this instrument" she said, holding her forked stick. "This is what I use on a regular basis and I can assure you that it works".

"What about the rod that some dowsers use?" Danelle asked her.

"Rods may also be used. For those familiar with Moses in the Bible, it says that he struck a rock with a rod and water poured forth. Well, Moses was no magician but I suspect he was a dowser." Chuckles were heard through the auditorium.

"Could you explain to us how dowsing first came to this country"?

"After America was discovered, there were many dowsers among the first immigrants to set foot in Canada. These folks were looked upon as indispensable people. There could never have been colonies formed and certainly no towns built without a large amount of water being available. When habitable sites were discovered, it wasn't always close to a body of water; therefore water had to be located underground".

"That certainly makes a lot of sense Jordyn. Do you mind telling us how you found out about your own dowsing ability"?

"I was thirteen years old when Dad hired a driller to dig our well. The digger got out of his truck and walked straight to a willow tree. Using his pocket knife, he cut himself a forked stick and proceeded to find water. Palms up and elbows held close to his sides, he walked around our property. He told Dad he was sorry but there was no water in that immediate area. He then walked toward our driveway. He was about twenty feet from the house when all of a sudden, the wooden stick turned downward, pulling his arms hard. His face lit up as he looked at me and Dad and then said : "Now, here is water and lots of it!"

He stood for a minute and the stick bobbed up and down so many times. He told Dad how many feet of drilling was needed and how many gallons per minute we could expect to draw from our well if Dad decided to let him drill in the middle of our driveway. After a few minutes reflection, Dad told him to go ahead and the drilling began. Half an hour later, we had an overflow and a lot of applauding neighbors who had gathered to watch".

"That is an incredible story Jordyn. Then what happened"?

"The driller jumped out of his truck and asked Dad if he had ever tried dowsing, to which Dad replied no, he never had. He handed him the stick and told him to try it, but nothing happened. The men and even the women who had gathered in our driveway all gave it a try but to no avail. All of a sudden, the driller looked at me and said

I might as well try it too. Being a shy thirteen year old, I was kind of hanging back but my mind was captivated by what was taking place.

A little hesitant, I finally took the forked stick and walked over to the spot he indicated. I had just taken a few steps when the stick took on a life of its own! All eyes were on me as I tried to turn the stick upward, but I couldn't no matter how hard I tried. Dad and our neighbors looked at me in amazement while the driller said, "Sir, you just got yourself a dowser!" No need to add that I was hooked that day and have been dowsing ever since".

The applause became thunderous! After they had quieted down, J. D. asked Jordyn if there was any scientific explanation for this phenomena and she answered that as far as she knew, there was none.

"Despite the sophistication of the instruments used by experts, there is no sure way of locating water in a certain spot without bringing in a dowser. Their success cannot be equaled. You also have to keep in mind that to this day, electricity is still a theory".

"It is, isn't it?" Danelle asked. She wanted to hear more on the subject, but she had to find out if the fans felt the same way. Turning to the audience, she asked, "Does anyone have a question for Jordyn"?

A young adult stood up and someone went up to him with a microphone.

"Does this ability to find water have anything to do with your faith"?

"Absolutely none," Jordyn replied. "The dowser's religious beliefs have nothing to do whatsoever with his or her ability to detect water. You either have the ability to find water or you don't. Unfortunately, there remains a lot of skepticism regarding this subject".

"Does anyone else have a question?"

An older gentleman stood up. "It's interesting that you've mentioned dowsing as a way of finding landmines. Is it being used for that purpose at this point in time?"

"I really don't know, but I do know that during World War 2, a certain troop was paralysed into inactivity due to landmines. One of the soldiers, described as being a quiet individual, asked his command officer what was holding them up. He learned they were being held up because of landmines and asked permission to dowse. His request was granted. He took a length of barbed wire, twisted it into a Y and proceeded to dowse. Needless to say, no soldiers were lost due to landmines at that particular location for the duration of that war. This account came from my grandfather who witnessed it as a young soldier".

"Thank you so much Jordyn for explaining to us what dowsing is all about. I know that I have been enlightened on that subject. How about you out there"?

A resounding 'yes' came from one end of the auditorium to the other. Jordyn Chamberlain was escorted back to her seat and the show went on.

CHAPTER 21

Lately, Joel's mind had been preoccupied with Ron Carpenter's tea leaf reading. He made himself a mental note to discuss it with Danelle as soon as he got home. She was getting supper ready when he walked through the front door and she knew something was on his mind as soon as he set his foot inside the kitchen. But, as always, he looked to see if Arielle was sleeping, which she was. So, he brushed a kiss on her forehead and one on Danelle's cheek.

"How is my second favourite girl"?

"I'm doing just great but how about you love? You look preoccupied".

When Joel told her he couldn't shake Ron Carpenter's tea leaf reading from his mind, she admitted having the same train of thoughts. They agreed that maybe it was time to give Mr. Carpenter a call. After they had finished supper, Joel dialed his number.

"Mr. Carpenter, this is Joel Harmon. How have you been"?

"The best, no complaints whatsoever. And you and the Mrs."?

"We're doing very well, thank you. There is now a little person residing with us whose name is Arielle and she's very much a little girl".

"Congratulation! I'm sure she's beautiful, like her mother".

"She is. Danelle and I were wondering if you're still interested in appearing on one of our shows to enlighten people about tea-cup reading"?

"Of course I'm still interested. I was wondering when you were going to get around to asking me. Was there a particular day you had in mind? Only reason I'm asking is because I'm planning to go visit my brother Don in the not too distant future".

"How about, let me see, the last Tuesday of this month? We have a show scheduled on the West Side of the city. I forgot to ask you where you live".

"Oh, not far, it's in a subdivision just outside Quispamsis. I can get to the West Side in twenty minutes".

"Great! We'll get back to you with the exact date and the location of the building where the show will be held. I think people will be very interested in learning about tea-cup reading".

"You have to remember to keep it straight Mr. Harmon, it's not tea-cup reading, but rather, tea leaf reading".

"Of course, Mr. Carpenter. I'll do my best not to forget that".

"Call me Ron," he replied.

******

On Tuesday, January 28, the school auditorium on Saint John's west side was jam packed. When the time came for introducing their special guest, J. D. called Ron Carpenter up on stage. He seemed very much at ease in front of an audience. Danelle couldn't help but admire him and wondered if he had any experience in public speaking.

"Mr. Carpenter, Ron, what can you tell us about your ability to read tea leaves? Was it inherited or is it a learned trade, so to speak"?

"Ladies and gentlemen," he began, "first, let me explain something. It's very important for you to understand that tea leaf reading is not a magic trick and it certainly isn't anything evil. Although we don't know what the future holds for us, it doesn't mean that it doesn't already exist in the non-physical world, even though it hasn't yet occurred in our physical world. This phenomenon has intrigued human beings since the dawn of time. How many of you know the meaning of the word 'Prophecy'"?

Most of the fans just looked at each other and frowned.

"That's what I thought. Yet," he continued, "prophesy has always existed. There have always been people who were able to predict future events. For example, Joseph, the young man in the Bible who was sold by his brothers for a few pieces of silver, was a prophet who foresaw the future through his dreams, while Nostradamus had his own way of making predictions that spanned over several centuries. Among others, the popular Edgar Cayce also made thousands of accurate predictions. Another example is the three Wise Men in the Christmas story. Did you ever think of them as being seers or prophets? People who relied on the stars for guidance were referred to as astronomers but I tend to think of them as astrologists. After all, they accurately pinpointed the location of the new born King as was prophesized in the Old Testament by examining the stars. Herod relied on these men to find a baby who, supposedly would become king, and out of jealousy, King Herod ordered him killed, unsuccessfully I might add.

So as you can see, there have been many people throughout history who have learned how to 'peek' into the future. Although Herod himself didn't have that ability, he found a way to deceive the wise men into telling him about their findings in the stars. But by being the wise men that they were, they outsmarted him by warning the parents of baby Jesus about Herod after realizing the baby was special. While astrologists or astronomers see the future in the stars, I see mine in tea leaves".

"Interesting! How else can you enlighten us on this subject Ron? Tell us how you acquired your ability to read tea leaves".

"An old Indian Chief taught me all that I know about tea leaf reading. He was one of the best readers I've ever known or heard of. My intention is to pass on this knowledge to this generation before it's too late, as I'm not getting any younger you know" he said, winking at the audience. Addressing the fans once again, he said "Tea leaf reading is a skill nearly anyone can master if they set their mind to it. Friends and family members can have hours of enjoyment by reading each other's tea leaves. It was great entertainment before television and computer games were invented. A package of loose tea is cheap compared to an electronic game". The audience readily agreed.

"You may even do your own reading. My Dad did it often after I showed him how it was done. He became very intrigued with what could be observed in the bottom of an empty tea cup. Since that day, he has pointed out to me on many occasions that the more knowledge one can have about the future, the better one is able to deal with certain circumstances or situations. It made sense to me, does it make sense to you Mrs. Harmon?" he asked, looking at Danelle.

"It makes a lot sense to me also." Turning to the audience, she said "This is indeed a very interesting topic, don't you agree? I was fortunate enough to have Mr. Carpenter do a reading for me a few months ago. It proved to be very enlightening to say the least! What else can you tell our listeners Ron"?

"I'd like to explain the reason tea leaf reading works".

"Please, go ahead," Danelle told him.

"Each person radiates a powerful energy field called an aura. This is a fact that can be proven by using Kirlian photography. A person's aura extends about three feet in every direction. Each person's aura is unique, just as every person is unique. Now consider this; every cell in a person's body contains one hundred percent of the information about that person's past, present and future. Not only that, which is amazing enough, but every cell in the body also contained a hologram of the universe. It is up to each one of us to retrieve that information if we have the means to do so. As I've pointed out to you earlier, there are different ways of glancing into the future, ways of retrieving such information. One way is by reading tea leaves".

"Tea leaves seem to be one substance that is easily influenced by exposing it to a person's aura. The leaves will cluster to symbolically record information coming from the exposure to that person's unique aura. It is always more effective if the person prepares his or her own cup of tea, which can then be read by the person himself or by someone else. And believe me, it works! I'm not saying that tea leaf reading is the most accurate form of presaging, however, a more powerful method requires disciplined training. Tea leaf reading is fun, requires very little effort on the part of the reader except having an open mind and a spirit of adventure".

He looked toward J. D. to see if his allotted time was up. J.D. took a step forward. "My dear people, what do you think of Mr. Carpenter's tea-leaf reading

ability?" he asked the fans who responded with roaring applause.

"As one last word of advice for anyone considering

reading tea leaves, what would that word be Mr. Carpenter, I mean Ron"?

"I can assure them that if done properly, according to instructions, tea leaf reading will be about 80% accurate with sometimes startling revelations. The readings are for a twelve month period and one cup of tea is needed for every answer sought after. Bottom line: one question asked, one cup of tea to be consumed. Two questions asked, two cups of tea to drink. Thus, it can become quite time consuming if you want the answer to a series of questions, involving quite a few trips to the washroom"!

The delighted audience broke into laughter and waves of applause reverberated through the auditorium as Ron continued; "There are books available to inform you what different symbols mean, that is the different forms that appear on the bottom of the cup being read. One such book has been written by William W. Hewitt. This book contains all the information you'll need to get started. Also, a clean cup and saucer should always be used. Notice that I said 'cup' and not 'mug'. Mugs make it nearly impossible to properly disperse the tea leaves. I also recommend that you use only loose tea opposed to opening a tea bag, which contains ground tea and has a tendency to 'clump' rather than form a pattern. Sweetener or milk products should never be used either as it can produce sticky residue, thus giving the reader inaccurate information".

"If I may interrupt you for a second," Danelle asked Ron, "could you quickly tell the fans what to do after the half a teaspoon of loose tea leaves, to be exact, is placed in the cup and the boiling water is poured over it"?

"Sure. Gently swirl your tea around your cup as you drink all the liquid, so as to make sufficient contact to send your energy to the tea leaves. Place the palm of your hand over the top of your cup for about two minutes. Then, turn your cup upside down in the saucer and let it drain on a paper towel. Don't be concerned if you lose a few tea leaves. The remaining leaves will still contain valid information. The reader will now turn the cup right side up and start reading. The tea leaves are always read in a clockwise fashion, beginning at the left edge of the cup handle. Instead of a twelve hour clock, think of the cup as a twelve month calendar. Now the fun begins"!

"Thank you so much Mr. Carpenter. I'm sure everyone has learned valuable information tonight about tea leaf reading. As for myself, I have found it extremely entertaining and I plan on trying my hand at it in the near future".

J.D. looked over at Tom and nodded his head. After shaking Ron Carpenter's hand he added "Tom will see you to your seat."

"Thank you for having me on your show J. D. and you too Mrs. Harmon," he said, before following Tom up the aisle to his seat.

The show continued with the fans expecting and looking for more entertainment which J. D. would provide, as always.

CHAPTER 22

Baby Arielle was a joy to be around and her Mom and Dad enjoyed every minute of her presence in their life. What a difference a tiny human could make! Danelle and Joel thought they were happy before Arielle was born, but they soon discovered that there was no comparison to becoming a parent. One night, after Joel had finished feeding Arielle her bottle and she was asleep for the night, he became strangely quiet and somewhat pensive looking. Danelle put her arm around his shoulder and whispered, "a penny for your thoughts or would a penny cover it?"

"I've been thinking a lot in the past few days. How

would you feel if I went back to college for a year? With the degree I already have, a year is all I'd need to be able to apply for the Hospital Administrator's job that's coming up in the fall of next year. My intuition is pulling me strongly in that direction".

"How do you know about that job honey? I've just heard about it yesterday from my assistant. She called to see how I was coping with my motherly duties."

"I read about it in this morning's paper. Of course, it would mean less time

to spend with you and Arielle so, be honest, what do you think"?

"Hon, you know I'd support you all the way, but wouldn't the J.D. Harmon show suffer? It wouldn't leave you much time to plan and organize your shows, would it? I know Tom is very efficient, but all the same, your input is needed".

"You're right, and I've thought about that too," Joel replied. Before he had a chance to say anything further,

Danelle's eyes widened and she exclaimed, "You want to give it up! What made you suddenly decide to do that honey?"

"It's not so sudden; it's been on my mind for quite some time. I feel that the work of J. D. Harmon has been accomplished. Do you understand what I mean Sweets"?

"Of course I do! Remember, it's me, Danelle you're talking to. I understand perfectly why you feel the way you do. There has been 'minute thoughts' going through my head as well. You were unknowingly passing them on to me. Joel dear, I knew that sooner or later, when the time was right, you were going to tell me about it. It's your decision to make honey, as this will affect the rest of your life. The J.D. Harmon show is all you know. Whatever you decide, I'll stand by you. Why don't we sleep on it and discuss it further in the morning".

"Good idea. Thank you, Sweets for understanding me when anyone else would think I was losing it. Right now, my biggest concern is how it will affect Arielle. She's only a couple of months old now but she'll be over a year old before I'm finished studying, considering I'll be accepted first term and, I won't know that until I make some inquiries which I plan on doing first thing in the morning".

"I really don't think this will have a negative effect on Arielle. But what about Tom? Have you considered what this will mean for him? He will no longer have a job".

"Tom would appreciate you're being so concerned about him, but he informed me a couple of weeks ago that he was thinking about an early retirement. He plans to embark on a world cruise, something he's always dreamed about and saved for. So, he certainly won't be shocked by the news, he'll probably find it helpful in coming to a decision. I'll talk to him about it tomorrow. Let's go to bed".

******

The following morning, while the coffee was

percolating, Danelle asked Joel if he thought she should consider taking a leave of absence after her maternity leave was over. "Would it make it easier for you knowing that I was home with Arielle?" As if baby Arielle had heard her name being spoken, she let out a wail.

"I guess she's ready for breakfast, wouldn't you say? Warm up her bottle while I go in and change her diaper. Our discussion is now over" she said, looking at Joel with a smile illuminating her whole face. "We know who the boss around here don't we?" After she was back in the kitchen holding a dry and much happier baby, Joel handed her the warmed bottle of milk then placed a tender kiss on Arielle's forehead.

"What are we having for breakfast? Do you want me to make French toast?"

"Sounds good to me but first, check the refrigerator to make sure we have some syrup. French toast without syrup is no good".

"Your sweet tooth is acting up, is it?" he asked while

opening the fridge door. "Yes, there is enough syrup for both of us. French toast, here we come" he said, juggling a couple of eggs. Arielle's eyes were following her father's every move, so that when he juggled the eggs one more time, she broke into a big grin, which Joel didn't miss.

"Look Danelle, she's smiling! Did you see it? She was really smiling! That was her first smile. Wow, she is some smart kid! And I think she smiled at me. Come on Arielle, smile again for daddy." By this time, Danelle was hysterical and Arielle had decided she wasn't going to smile again. Her breakfast was more important.

"That was precious! Can you imagine, only two months old and she's already smiling. That's my girl, charming and happy with a sense of humour. She's beautiful, isn't she? God has blessed us with this adorable child. Thank you Danelle for bringing her into the world".

"I did have some help you know, but when you put it this way honey, I can't help but feel very blessed indeed"!

"To get back to our conversation, I honestly don't think

it's necessary for you to take a leave of absence. We've already inquired and found a very good daycare for Arielle and I don't think it would be good for you to be away from your work too long, and then who knows, you might have to take another year's maternity leave".

"You've got it all planned haven't you? Did you hear that Arielle, Daddy is planning to give you a brother or a sister to play with. How clever of him"!

"Very clever I would say," he said before planting a kiss on Danelle's lips.

"Joel! Look at the clock! We've been talking for over an hour. You have to get to the office to sort things out."

"Yes, I suppose I have to go, as much as I'm enjoying myself here." He brushed a kiss on Arielle's and then Danelle's cheek and headed out for the office where he found Tom already at work. Tom glanced up from a bunch of papers spread out in front of him.

"Good morning boss, how is everything going this

morning? Did Arielle let you sleep to your heart's content or did she pull at your heart's strings?"

"Pulling at my heart's strings would describe it best. She is such a gem though! When she looks at me with those big blue eyes, she gets my attention, believe me. Would you believe that she smiled for the first time this morning? You should have seen it"!

"I'll bet no other kid can do that, I mean smile like that," Tom teased Joel. He had never seen such a proud father. It made him wonder what it would be like to have a child of his own but life as a father had passed him by. It was too late for regrets now. He had enough nieces and nephews to spoil and now, he could adopt Arielle as one of them. J D.'s voice broke through his thoughts.

"Tom, we have serious business to discuss".

"If looks say anything, I guess we have. What is it boss"?

"How close would you say you are from retirement"?

"What does that have to do with anything"?

"It has everything to do with it. Have you thought about it enough to give me an answer now or do you need some more time before you make a decision"?

"You've taken me by surprise boss, but I think I can answer your question right now. I could retire as soon as you've found someone to replace me, how is that?"

Joel jumped up and slapped Tom on the shoulder.

"Hey man, you don't know how happy you've made me"!

"But I thought I was doing a good job as your manager".

"You were, I mean you are! One more show my friend, that's all we need and the J. D. Harmon Show will be a thing of the past".

"My God, what brought that on? Is it something I did?"

"No. No, don't ever think that. It's been on my mind for awhile now, and last week when you mentioned a possible early retirement, it all fell into place. I talked to

Danelle about it last night and this morning. I explained to her how I'd like to further my education and go into business administration and she wholeheartedly supports me. She is such an understanding partner".

"You can say that again. Any other woman would have tried to knock some sense into you. What brought all this on anyway"?

"Nothing in particular. I just need to follow a different path in life's journey and make sure I don't have any regrets at the end of the road. All that matters is that Danelle understands. So my friend, we'll have to put our energy into this one last show. I hope we can attract a young audience, an audience that is open to the message I want to leave".

"I'll think of a way to do it. It shouldn't be too hard".

"Then, I'm off to take care of something else" Joel said on his way out. "I have an appointment with a university professor at 1 o'clock this afternoon." From where Joel was standing, he could see the University of New

Brunswick beckoning. "And I think I can do it" he added as an afterthought.

"I hope everything works out for you J. D., you deserve it," Tom muttered as Joel closed the door behind him.

*****

Joel came out of his meeting wearing a big smile on his face. He had been accepted first term, which was beginning in September. He drove home, whistling all the way. He could call Danelle on his cell and give her the good news, but he chose to wait and tell her in person. His life's path was turning at a sharp angle but he knew it was the right angle. He could feel it in his bones!

CHAPTER 23

A couple of days later, Joel switched the T.V. on to watch Live at Five. His attention was abruptly summoned when he heard 'Fifth Brazilian Carnival coming to Halifax, Nova Scotia in June'. It went on to say that the carnival master was a well known acrobat from Rio de Janeiro. Joel was still processing that information in his head when the phone started ringing. Danelle came in the room holding the baby against her shoulder. "Do you mind answering the phone honey? I don't want Arielle to get a chill, she just came out of her bath".

"No problem, give me a second." He hopped to the nearest telephone.

"Hello, you have reached the Harmon's residence".

"I am glad to find you at home Mr. Harmon. My name is Juanito Junqueira. I am presently calling from Toronto. I am in your country for five weeks doing a carnival tour. I am the leader of the carnival and I would like to speak with you about my little nephew if I may"?

A light bulb lit up in Joel's head and his whole body became alert to what was being said to him on the other end of the telephone.

"I would be delighted to speak to you about your nephew, please go on".

"I have reason to believe that you and your wife may have met my nephew last year while you were visiting our country".

"It's very possible, what is his name"?

"His name is Mohad and he is a remarkable child. I have

decided to bring him along on these four major Canadian city tours".

"Let me get this straight, you are the leader of the Fifth Brazilian Carnival?" is this correct?"

"This is true."

"Would one of those city tours happen to be in Halifax, Nova Scotia"?

"You are very correct sir, but how do you know this, if I may ask"?

"I have just finished seeing it announced on the A.T.V. Live at Five program. How can I help you Mr. Junqueira is it"?

"I was wondering if it was realistic to plan a visit with you and your wife before our tour is finished and we have to return to Brazil".

"Are you asking me to meet with you and Mohad"?

"That is what I wish to do".

"Do you realize, Mr. Junqueira, that this has been our wish ever since our unusual meeting with Mohad, to be able to meet that little boy once again. We just didn't think it would ever be possible to get in touch with him. I'm a little confused as to how this came about".

"When you were speaking with Mohad and his mother, who is my sister, I spoke a few words with you. I didn't see any need to say more, for you were only a couple of tourists passing through our town. But then, I saw your show on television one night while we were touring the United States and I realized that you were the couple who were so interested in Mohad that day".

"You mentioned that you are calling from Toronto, when are you planning to come to Halifax"?

"In four weeks time, from June 12th. to the 15th. On the last day of the carnival, the day before we depart for Rio de Janeiro, Mohad and I could try to go find you in New Brunswick".

"Mr. Junqueira, you don't know how happy you've made me. There is no need to worry about finding us in New Brunswick, we will come to you. My wife will be thrilled! Keep in touch with us and when the day comes, in three weeks, we'll be in Halifax to welcome you. Say hello to Mohad for us O.K."?

"I will call two days prior to the day we leave for our tour to Halifax. Will that give you enough time"?

"That will be perfect. We'll be waiting for your call".

As soon as Danelle heard 'Fifth Brazilian Carnival' it was enough for her to come to her own conclusion. She was just starring at Joel, and whatever she heard being said on this end of the telephone had left her flabbergasted. "Oh my God, is it really Mohad?" she asked after Joel had hung up. "What's going on?"

"That was Mohad's uncle, head of a carnival that is touring our country. He's the man we met in Brazil, the one who told us about Mohad being able to communicate with animals and seem unconcerned about the whole thing".

"How did he get our phone number"?

"He saw our televised show while they were touring the U.S. He thought he recognized us as being the tourists who had been talking to Mohad and his mother that day.

By the way, Mohad's mom is Mr. Junqueira's sister, so he

jotted down our phone number from the T.V. screen. Isn't

it amazing"!

"Honey, do you think this is just a coincidence"?

"No, I do not. First, I don't believe in coincidence

and second, it's too grand of a scheme to just 'happen'. It

had to have been planned by someone with much greater

intelligence than the human mind, someone who knows

all things, and someone who loves all his children like no

other and who listens to their prayers of supplication. I

believe that our prayer has been heard and answered by

the all powerful God who listens to the needs of all his

creatures".

"So do I, although it's beyond my comprehension Joel.

But I am so happy! Aren't we baby girl?" she asked little

Arielle who was gazing adoringly at her mom.

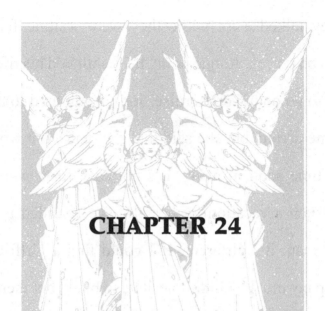

CHAPTER 24

As plans were being made for the last J.D. Harmon Show, Tom found an excuse to phone Jordyn Chamberlain. He wanted to invite her out for supper that evening to discuss her next appearance while making it a pleasurable business meeting. Of course he was only kidding himself. He had yearned to see Jordyn since her last appearance on the show. She accepted and as soon as he found himself sitting across the table from her, he felt as though he had found his best friend. The feeling was mutual because Tom had been on Jordyn's mind ever since she had appeared on the last J.D. Harmon show.

They talked a lot while they were waiting for their food to be served. At one point, he mentioned his life-long dream to go on a world cruise. Jordyn admitted to having the same dream, but she said that she realized it wouldn't be anytime soon, if ever. "It's not easy for a woman to go on such a vacation by herself" she confided to Tom. "For a man, it's different. If I could find a girlfriend to accompany me, I wouldn't hesitate to book, but there isn't anyone willing or available it seems. I've been working for almost twenty years and all the while, saving for a cruise that may never happen".

"You're serious about this, aren't you"?

"Oh yes, I'm dead serious," Jordyn replied, laughing at the way he was looking at her. "Why, don't you approve of a woman going on a cruise by herself?"

"It's not that, I was thinking of another possibility. You are hesitant to go because you feel unsafe, don't you?"

"Well yes, that's part of the reason".

"How would you feel about going if there was someone looking out for you, I mean other than a girlfriend"?

"If you're asking what I think you're asking, the answer is no, I wouldn't go on a cruise with a man, unless, of course, it was my brother, my husband or maybe a serious boyfriend". She was a little offended by his suggestion. "Does that answer your question Tom?"

"Plain as day! What about a friend who happens to be male"?

"And, may I ask who that friend could be?" Jordyn was beginning to feel a little uncomfortable and she could feel her cheeks burning.

"I'm sorry; I didn't mean to embarrass you Jordyn. I am going on that world cruise in a couple of months. I'm taking an early retirement soon. There is nothing and no one to hold me back. I certainly wouldn't mind keeping an eye out for you if you were to decide to embark on the same cruise".

"I don't know, I honestly don't know Tom," she replied, flustered by his suggestion.

"Don't answer just yet, give it some thought. It's a 50 day cruise and if nothing else, we'd be company for each other. Even a cruise ship could be a lonely place if you didn't have anybody to talk with." Looking up, he continued "As the saying goes, saved by the bell," as the waiter arrived with their food. "Enjoy your meal and we'll resume our conversation later."

"O.K.," Jordyn replied, her color returning to normal.

When their meal was done and they had finished discussing the business that had brought them there in the first place, Tom asked her if she would like to attend the Elton John Concert that was scheduled to take place in three weeks time. Again, it took her by surprise. She only hesitated long enough to remind herself that she liked Elton John too, so why not go with him? He seemed like a very nice man. So she said yes, she would love to go to the concert with him. Tom was so sure she would say no that he let out the breath he'd been holding.

"That's great! We'll go out for dinner first, that is, if you'd like to do that".

"That sounds good to me, but I really think we should be leaving. The owner has been looking at the clock off and on for the past fifteen minutes".

"Has he really? My gosh, we wouldn't want him to have to work overtime." He helped her with the light jacket she was wearing.

On the way home, she wondered how old Tom might be but she couldn't bring herself to ask him. She would mention it to Danelle, whom she had gotten to know quite well these past few months. She would also ask her what she thought of Tom's suggestion for the cruise and inquire about his age then. Danelle would know, for Tom had been working with Joel for years.

The silence was making her nervous, so she was grateful when Tom popped a C.D. in the car stereo. She closed her eyes and tried to relax but she found it almost impossible.

She was way too conscious of the man sitting next to her.

She looked sideways, but she couldn't tell what was on his

mind as his lip curled into a smile.

CHAPTER 25

The following day, Joel walked in the door with a happy smile on his face.

"It's all arranged," he announced. "We will be meeting with Mohad and his uncle after the last carnival performance. He has someone looking after the boy when he works. I feel so lucky to finally be able to see and speak at length with little Mohad".

. "You are so right honey and I think you're a very lucky man. You have a daughter who adores you and a wife who is head over heels in love with you. I think that's pretty darn lucky, don't you think so baby girl"?

Arielle was looking from one to the other when suddenly, she gave them a big toothless grin.

"I had a visitor today" Danelle told Joel. "What do you know about a certain world cruise?"

"Are you talking about the cruise that Tom is planning to go on in a couple of months? Did he come to you asking for advice"?

"No, he didn't but Jordyn Chamberlain did." At the blank look he gave her, Danelle continued, "Do you mean to tell me that Tom didn't mention to you that he encouraged Jordyn to go on the same cruise so he could keep an eye out for her?"

"You're kidding! Who told you he did that"?

"Jordyn told me. She wanted to know if Tom could be trusted and also how old he was. Isn't that interesting"?

"Well, is she thinking of going with him"?

"Not 'with' him, but she's thinking of going on the same cruise, yes. He convinced her she would feel safer knowing someone she knew was on board".

"I think maybe Tom is feeling that he missed something out of life, wouldn't you say"?

"Now Joel, don't go assuming things. He only suggested he could keep an eye on her, nothing else".

"You may be right Sweets, but something tells me his heart and her heart might be involved before the cruise is over. It's strange that he hasn't mentioned anything to me though. I remember getting the impression that he was fond of Jordyn the last time she appeared on our show".

"So did I, so I advised Jordyn to go for it. Tom is trustworthy and he will make sure she's safe the whole time," Danelle replied, leading the way into the kitchen.

"Here baby girl," she said, handing Arielle over to Joel, "go see your daddy while mommy dishes out the food. But none for you my little princess, because you shouldn't be hungry with all the baby food you ate".

"This is why you're getting so heavy, you eat so much," Joel declared, all the while cradling his daughter in his arms and covering her forehead with butterfly kisses. Arielle gave him a huge grin.

"So, do you think Jordyn will take your advice and go on that cruise"?

"I got the distinct impression that she was seriously considering it. I assured her that Tom could be trusted. Did you know that she is forty one years old? That surprised me, she looks so much younger! She was a little concerned that Tom was fifty three though".

"See? That is proof that she may be more interested in him than she lets on. I hope she does decide to go on that cruise".

*****

Meanwhile, the culmination of the J.D. Harmon Show was closing in. There were few days remaining before he and Tom would launch the biggest advertising endeavor to ensure for a successful and entertaining show. The fact that it would be the last one would be kept secret until the end. Otherwise, the Imperial Theatre wouldn't have adequate space to hold the many fans who would want to attend.

The date was set for May 1st. May Day seemed to be the perfect time to end a period of one's life that had been so fulfilling. Danelle helped with the preparations. The three of them spent a whole evening suggesting, compromising and eliminating possible candidates to appear for that memorable last show. At the end of their meeting, they believed they had found the best assortment of special people possible. One of those special people was a young man who had never appeared on any of the J. D. Harmon shows but someone who was guaranteed to empress their audience. His name was Rémi Boudreau from the Moncton area. Rémi had appeared on stage many times to entertain children especially. Having been interested in magic since he was very young, Rémi hoped that one day, he might be recognized as a famous magician. His parents were very supportive of his magic acts and encouraged him to bring it to full potential. For this reason, he had decided to call J.D. Harmon and asked him if he would be interested in seeing what he was capable of doing. J.D. had readily agreed, one of the reasons being that he was such a young magician, still in his teenage years. Magicians were usually older than that.

What had intrigued J.D. the most was Rémi's ability to bend metal by using only the power of his mind. J.D. and Danelle had interviewed him together and had been very impressed by the young man. Besides performing magic tricks, he was also a comedian who incorporated his magic as an enhancement to his act, or you could say he was a magician who incorporated comedy as a way of holding people's attention. Whichever way people saw him, they liked him, for he was definitely an entertainer. The older generation was intrigued with his card tricks while the children were amazed at his pulling multiple doves out of a hat or a box.

Danelle had suggested to Joel and Tom that maybe they should let Rémi do the opening act on May 1st, even before J.D. did any of his usual mental challenges. She sensed that one day, this young man might take center stage and become as popular as J.D. himself. As it is often the case, one door closes only to let another one open. This might just be the 'cosmic' opportunity for Rémi Boudreau of Saint-Antoine, N.B.

Another person they decided to invite was Jeremy Melvin. They knew it would be impossible to invite everyone who had made an appearance on one of J.D. Harmon's show, therefore Connor Harrigan had to be left out. If Erika Latimer was willing to come, they felt strongly about inviting her. Ron Carpenter would be asked to describe tea-leaf reading. Tina Stevenson, although an interesting candidate, would have to be left out also. One guest who would be invited was Lisa d'Entremont so she could explain to the fans all about Reiki treatments.

There was room for seven guests, so they decided that

Jordyn Chamberlain would probably hold the interest of their last audience by demonstrating her ability to find water underground. Tom's eyes lit up at the mere mentioning of her name and readily agreed to add her on their list of guests. Danelle and Joel looked at each other and grinned. There would be no argument there! And, of course, the "Amazing Twins' would have to be incorporated somehow.

Without a doubt, Josie Quinlan would be asked to appear as one of the special guest and Danelle wanted to tell the audience one more time how grateful she was to have been made to return to her body after her crossing over, for she couldn't imagine a world without Arielle and Joel in it. Finally, Joel himself would give a final message to his fans that he had come to think of as his friends.

The calls were made to confirm that everyone invited would be able to attend. Erika, as well as Josie and her mom and dad had the greatest distance to travel, but they didn't seem to mind one little bit. 'It would give them an opportunity to visit baby Arielle' is how they had put it. Everything was arranged to the last detail. The tickets went on sale two weeks prior to the event and as usual, all tickets were 'sold out' in the first week of being available. It looked like it was going to be another successful night of entertainment.

CHAPTER 26

As planned, on the night of May 1ˢᵗ, the Imperial Theatre was filled to capacity. At the trumpet sound, the curtains opened and J.D. introduced himself and Danelle, who looked stunning in a beautiful long, light blue evening gown but unlike past times, she came out holding Arielle in her arms. Everyone stood as they saw the baby. When Joel could make himself heard above the applause, he said, "We know which one of us is the most popular. This is Arielle, and at the risk of sounding prejudice, we think she is the most perfect and beautiful baby in the world.

Baby Arielle will be seven months old next week and we cannot imagine our life without her".

"Without a doubt, she is our pride and joy!" Danelle added, as she handed Arielle over to Joel and went on to introduce their very special guest who was Rémi Boudreau, from St-Antoine, New Brunswick. The fans reacted with more applause yet. Some of the fans knew of Rémi the magician through acquaintances while others recognized him after attending his magic show in person. Rémi had become interested in magic at the tender age of nine or ten, although he hadn't performed in public until after he turned thirteen years of age. His parents supported him and even encouraged him to pursue his dream of becoming a magician, hopeful that one day, he would be a well known one.

As always, his Mom and Dad had given him a hand with transporting his 'tools' on stage. A magician thinks of his props as tools, just as a carpenter thinks of his hammer and saw as tools. Besides doing magic tricks, Rémi also had a great sense of humor and enjoyed making people laugh. So, Rémi the comedic-magician showed the audience what he was able to do and was rewarded by their enthusiastic response. He made them roar with laughter as he told a few jokes while getting his props just the right way, after which he became serious. He did the coin trick and the card trick, involving some of the kids in the front row. And then he did the short, loose strings that tie themselves together into a long rope, tricks that seemed to impress the audience enough, but his next act truly got their undivided attention. He picked up a dinner fork which he held up for all to see. Then, he asked J.D. if he would mind coming up to check the fork and make sure it was an ordinary dinner fork. After examining it closely, J.D. was convinced that it was just that, a table fork and said so to the audience before retreating to his seat.

Rémi then held the same fork between his fingers and asked the audience to be as quiet as possible and to keep watching his hand as he began to concentrate on the fork.

His whole arm seemed to vibrate as his concentration deepened. Before their very eyes, the fork started changing shape and in a few minutes, it no longer looked like a fork but like a fan, each pick of the fork evenly spread. It was truly amazing to witness the power that was being generated from Rémi's mind onto the metal fork.

We know that few human beings can control their minds in such a way as Rémi did in front of all those people. Slowly, his hand steadied, his face became relaxed in a smile and he handed the fanned fork to a person in the front row as a souvenir.

You could tell the crowd was truly impressed by the way they responded to the young magician's final act, the endless pulling of doves out of a hat. They showed their appreciation by giving Rémi a standing ovation! He bowed from the waist and turned toward J.D. and Danelle, beckoning them to come to the rescue, for he wasn't sure how to proceed any further. As they both reached the stage,

Danelle gave Rémi a hug while J.D. shook hands with him before addressing the audience.

"This talented young man has just proved to you that the body and the mind are continually intertwined. Each person is a masterpiece, a work of art whom some parts are still a mystery to be discovered, and the brain being undoubtedly the most complex. Thank you Rémi for showing us what power the mind has over matter". Danelle showed Remi to the dressing room while his mom and dad efficiently cleared the props off the stage. It was heart-warming to see a family work so well together. Being the middle child certainly hadn't had any negative effect on Rémi Boudreau. His whole family was very proud of him.

*****

The next guest to be introduced was Ron Carpenter, the well known tea leaf reader. Always at ease in front of a crowd, Ron shook hands with J.D. and waved to the audience. "Do I have a volunteer?" he asked. "Who would like to come up on stage for a demonstration on tea leaf reading?"

A man stood up and started walking toward the front. The man was led up on the stage at the same time as Danelle entered from the side entrance, pushing a tea cart in front of her. "The only thing required for you to do" Ron told the man, "is to drink the tea from this teacup, which is only half full before I can do a reading for you. I hope you like tea." While Ron was explaining to the fans what would be taking place, he asked for the name of his volunteer, "Léonce Doiron," the man replied.

"O.K. Léonce, are you positive you want to do this"?

"Yes Sir, I am. I can't wait to see what's going to appear in my cup." The tone of his voice revealed that Mr. Doiron had his doubt about the whole thing. Ron didn't lose any time as he sat across the table from Léonce.

"Let's begin then. While you drink your tea, hold the

cup with both hands, placing your palm over the rim like so, and concentrate on the tea leaves, got that"?

"Got it, no problem," Leonce replied while sipping his tea and grinning.

"When you're done, turn your cup upside down on this piece of paper towel in your saucer." Turning to the fans once more, he continued; "Tea leaves are receptive to the energy that is emitted from the person's body, in this case, from the hands of the person holding and drinking the cup of tea. Energy is generated from every cell in the human body and each cell contains information about that person's past, present and future. You may think that this is a tall order to accept but it is the truth or rather, what I believe to be the truth. You may accept it or leave it, that's entirely up to you." Turning to Mr. Doiron, he asked, "How is the tea drinking coming along Léonce? Does Mrs. Harmon make a good cup of tea?" he said, winking at the audience.

"Very good indeed," Léonce replied, "in fact, it was so good that I'm all done" he said looking inside his cup as he turned it upside down on the paper towel as advised by Ron at the beginning. Pulling his chair alongside Léonce, Ron gingerly picked up the tea cup and looked inside.

"We read a cup the way we examine a watch, clockwise. You may also think of the cup as being a round calendar." Pointing to something at the bottom of the cup he said, "Have you, by any chance, been pulling teeth?" The audience started to laugh but came to an abrupt stop when Léonce replied "Yes, I have extracted a few teeth in my career. I'm a dentist."

"Ah," replied Ron "that would explain it. Look at all the miniature teeth on the bottom left of your cup, the side which indicates the past. The opposite side of the handle indicates the present and the first thing that comes to my mind when I see a bell" he said, pointing to it, is a wedding. Will you be getting married soon or did you just get married?"

"My wife and I are here on our honeymoon. It's incredible that you can see that in my cup Mr. Carpenter"!

"I can see a lot more, but life wouldn't be half as exciting if we knew everything before it happened. Now, I will peek into your future for a brief moment. What do you make of this?" he asked, pointing to the far right of the cup.

"It looks like a swing or maybe a basinet".

"What do you suppose it means"?

"I have no idea. Maybe we'll be purchasing a home beside a playground or something," he joked.

"Maybe you will, but this is much more personal than that. How do you feel about becoming a father? Because, a basinet indicates a baby."

"A baby? I haven't really thought about it. When"?

"Sorry, that I cannot tell you. I can't give you a date but I can assure you that inside of a year, you will become a parent." The audience started clapping and Léonce was escorted back to his seat where he rejoined a very surprised wife!

J.D. thanked Ron Carpenter for the reading while

Danelle cleared the tea cart from the stage, making way for their next guest who happened to be Erika Latimer.

"I have another special guest tonight. Some of you may recall this young lady from a past performance. Please make welcome, all the way from Whitehorse, in the Yukon, the lovely Erika Latimer".

Erika came on stage with Danelle. She was even more beautiful than she had been the year before. She wore her long black hair in a braid which brought out her high cheekbones and perfectly arched eyebrows. And her beautiful smile had not gone un-noticed by Rémi who had met her backstage. He had been quite smitten by Miss Latimer, to say the least!

"Welcome back to Saint John, Erika. It's always a pleasure to have you here with us. Would you tell the audience, in your own words, why we think you're so special?" Laughing, she replied, "I certainly don't think of myself as being special. I'm an ordinary teenager who has been blessed with the ability to see and communicate with angels, especially guardian angels. I think everyone is special and unique, with a guardian angel to guide them if only they're willing to listen. I've always been able to communicate with mine, but for years, nobody knew. If it hadn't been for Mr. Harmon and his wife, I would probably still keep silent about it. Now, I can tell the whole world and they believe me." The interest ran high as Erika spoke about angels. At J.D.'s urging, she continued; "Angels are all around us, even at this moment. I hope that one day soon, everyone will be able to see them and experience their presence. I was told that the sole purpose for their existence is to protect humanity. That is the main reason the guardian angels were created. There are different ranks of angels, such as the Cherubims and the Seraphims. Some were created to sing heavenly praises; others were created to be 'helpers' and only come to us when summoned. They have been known through the centuries as 'Beings of Light' and also as 'Spirit Guides' and they love helping us, so when we acknowledge their presence, they rejoice all the more. They especially rejoice upon hearing the popular prayer 'Angel of God' which goes like this:

'Angel of God, my guardian dear, to whom God's love commits me here. Ever this day be at my side, to light and guard, to rule and guide, Amen'. This is a very simple but also very effective prayer. Whatever you do or however you think, I beg you never to ignore your guardian angel. Every human being has one of his own waiting to be called upon. Your life will be enriched if you learn to ask for your angel's protection and guidance".

Erika then took a step back, indicating that she was done.

"Thank you once again Erika, for sharing your knowledge of these heavenly beings called angels. When do you plan on returning to the Yukon"?

"I'm happy to say that I'm staying a bit longer this time, because I plan on moving to New Brunswick. Your province has made a big impression on me, Mr. Harmon.

I've applied to continue my studies in this area, so it all depends how things work out. I will keep in touch".

"I certainly hope so. That is great news! I wasn't expecting that".

Erika was escorted backstage and the next guest to be introduced was Jordyn Chamberlain. Jordyn had been asked to bring along her dowsing rod as there was a possibility she might be able to do a demonstration. Before she went on to explain how dowsing or divining was accomplished, she showed the audience a short video tape of herself having just found a water vein, the drillers busy and the water gushing out of the ground. By the reaction of the audience, they were interested in seeing how it was done. She set off to show them the procedure, which began by holding the forked piece of wood in both hands. She began walking back and forth across the stage, all the while explaining what she was doing. Once again, as had happened on other occasions, the stick began to pull downward. Jordyn asked J.D. if one of the fans would like to come up and experience for themselves, the energy coming from the stick. It didn't take long for someone to volunteer. With Tom's helpful hand, an elderly gentleman walked up the steps leading on stage, shook hands with J.D. and Danelle, then turned to Jordyn and told her how very fascinated he'd been by her dowsing. She asked his name, which was Andrew Merchant and invited him to take hold of the piece of wood.

"Hold it straight in front of you like so Mr. Merchant and see what happens."As soon as he touched the stick, it took on a life of its own!

"Wow! From past experience, I can say that you either have the gift of dowsing or you don't, and believe me Mr. Merchant, you've got it! I've never seen such a strong pull. Now, try to hold it steadier until it starts to bob up and down, indicating how many feet before water would be found if you were to dig in this exact spot." As predicted, the bobbing began and Jordyn started counting. As she reached a count of fifty, the bobbing stick began to slow down and before she reached sixty, it came to a stop.

"There, Mr. Merchant, fifty-eight feet below, give or take a few feet, you would have plenty of water for a well to be dug , given that it wouldn't be located under this theatre stage," she added. Loud chuckles came from the audience.

"You can feel confident that your dowsing ability will work when needed. Thank you for coming up to help me with my demonstration." She then went on to explain how else a person would use a dowsing rod, which seemed to impress everyone in attendance.

A moment later, J.D. and Danelle advanced closer and thanked both Mr. Merchant and Jordyn, who were then escorted off the stage. The fans showed their interest by the length of the applause they gave them. It was time for intermission and J.D. promised more of the same when they returned after the break. The curtains closed and ten minutes later, when they reopened, Danelle and J.D. came out as a family, baby Arielle Elisabeth snuggled in the arms of her daddy.

"Dear people, I have an announcement to make which makes us both sad and happy at the same time. I'm sorry to tell you that tonight is the last of The J.D. Harmon Show". That's all he was allowed to say before the audience started to shout, jumping to their feet, "No, you can't stop, we want you and Danelle and we want the show to go on!" As soon as he was able to insert a word in, J.D. added, "I really appreciate the fact that you like our show so much, but the time has come for Danelle and I to move forward. Remember the night I told you that there was a time for everything under the sun? Well dear people, that time for us, more so for 'me' has arrived. I plan to further my education beginning this coming September. During the past six years, I have done what my conscience has led me to do and now I have to move on. I feel that I have accomplished the first part of what God had in store for me. The other part being that of a husband and father will take the rest of my life to fulfill".

"I promise to help anyone who calls on me for advice based on my psychic capability. Having psychic abilities means having a clearer insight on certain matters. I'll refresh your memory with something I've told you over the years, that we are all born with psychic abilities but soon after birth, those abilities become 'out of reach' for most people. Very few, such as Erika Latimer, experience the presence of angels, but it doesn't mean they don't exist. As for myself and Danelle, some of our abilities have been restored to us while we were still in our teens, each of us having undergone near death experiences, myself as the result of a car accident and Danelle, from a certain illness. There is no doubt in my mind that the human race is still on a 'time out', at least for the time being. Once the Author of Life sees fit to liberate us, our privileges will be returned to us in full measure".

"When is that gonna be?" someone wanted to know.

"When will this take place? No one knows. At this point in time, I would say that the children of God are still in a rebellious state. Attitudes must change! Tonight, I'm asking you to live your life to the best of your ability, whether it is being a good brother or sister, a parent, a friend, a pastor, a doctor, a musician or a teacher, just give it your best shot. Look for the good in others instead of looking for the bad. Be thankful for what you have and for who you are. Be generous instead of greedy and be forgiving instead of holding a grudge. We have the power to move mountains one 'smile' at a time".

"Hurrah! Hurray!" came the response from his faithful fans. Still holding on to Danelle's hand and cradling his daughter, he continued; "The time has come to introduce you to our last two guests. The first one is a remarkable woman with the gift of healing. How many of you have heard of the art of Reiki?" A few hands shot up, but it was clear that not too many of them knew what Reiki was.

"Reiki has been practiced for centuries, in one form

or another. As part of their culture, the Chinese people believed in the healing of their sick using their own energy. Of course, like modern medicine today, it didn't always work. Therefore, it is with great respect that I introduce to you Lisa d'Entrement whom, I'm pleased to say, convinced my wife Danelle that the body can transfer healing energy to someone else in such a way that it can make pain disappear, even serious pain. Welcome to our show Lisa. I hope someone in our audience can benefit from your healing hands. Who wants to volunteer for this particular demonstration"?

A woman in her fifties stood up, telling J.D. that she would like to take part in the demonstration. Lisa asked her to make her way up to the stage and Tom made sure the woman was steady on her feet. Welcoming her at once, Lisa asked how long she had been suffering with a migraine. Amazed, the woman could only gasp at Lisa, asking her how she could tell her head was throbbing.

"Its part of my job," Lisa replied. "First, I looked to

determine what colour your aura was. For those who are not familiar with this expression, the aura is the energy emitted from each person's body. I see pain in colour, so it's plain for me to see that her head is viciously aching because the aura around her head is red, not as bright red as someone with a serious disease of the brain would have, but all the same, a dull red which indicates a migraine. For those who were fortunate enough to have never experienced a migraine, I can assure you that it can be very painful, excruciating even. Would you like to get rid of your migraine Ms"?

"My name is Caroline and yes, I would love to get rid of this migraine that has plagued me off and on for years".

"I can't promise you that it will never return, but we'll get rid of it for tonight at least. Please sit down comfortably Caroline and close your eyes. Good, now I will concentrate on the pain inside your head and if you begin to feel warmth penetrating your skull, don't panic. Just enjoy the feeling of wellbeing that will shortly follow it. If you're ready, I'll begin. You won't feel my hands because I will not be touching you".

Lisa extended her hands over Caroline's head as she concentrated deeply. All eyes were looking expectantly to see if they could notice anything different about Caroline's expression, but she remained calm. After a couple of minutes, Caroline jumped up off the chair and declared that her headache had disappeared! She looked at Lisa in wonder and asked how that was possible, for her head had been aching continually for the past two days.

"This is what I want people to understand, that the mind has great potential if only we knew how to use it the way it was intended. To you, it may seem like I've accomplished something out of the ordinary but to me, it's just part of my work day. Mrs. Harmon can confirm this because she was relieved of a nagging back ache while she was expecting her child. Mrs. Harmon, would you mind telling the audience what took place in your kitchen last fall?"

Coming from the sideline, Danelle said; "Certainly not, I would love to tell everyone what took place that day. I had an appointment with Miss d'Entrement one afternoon to determine if she would appear as a guest on our show, and as she began to explain what it was that she did, she stopped abruptly and asked me if my back was causing me discomfort, which it was. As with Caroline, she explained to me that the aura surrounding my lower back was a different colour than it should have been. She said it was pink instead of the well-being blue colour that surrounds a healthy body. She asked me to turn around for a few minutes when to my surprise, I began to feel heat penetrating my lower back. When I turned to look at her, she had her eyes closed and seemed to be concentrating deeply. Within minutes, the pain in my back was gone. You may believe what you like, but I believe that through the power of her mind, Lisa made my backache disappear".

"Thank you Mrs. Harmon, I appreciate having been invited to appear on your final show. I wish you the best in the future." Lisa d'Entremont was escorted down to her seat.

J.D. came to join Danelle and to introduce their very last guest.

"Ladies and gentlemen, as the saying goes, we've kept the best for last. It gives us great pleasure to introduce to you someone whom we have grown very close to".

Looking at Danelle, he motioned for her to take over.

"Her name is Josie Quinlan. Josie is five and a half years old and lives with her parents in Stratford, Ontario. Please make her welcome one more time." The clapping went on and on until J.D. held his hand up to appease them. Josie was looking from Danelle to Joel, then back to the audience.

"Josie dear, what can you show our fans tonight that will be of interest to them? Are you going to play an instrument or are you planning to maybe surprise us"?

"Mr. Harmon, I have been talking with Monica and Emily and we were having so much fun. They asked me to tell people something that they forgot to tell them earlier on. They asked me to relay this message, once the monarch butterflies begin migrating in the spring, it's only a matter of time before they discover milkweed in your garden so, and a good way to attract them is by planting milkweed as early as possible in the spring. In early summer, the female lays her eggs on the underside of milkweed leaves. Five days later, tiny caterpillars, also called larvae, emerge with yellow, black and white bands. They grow rapidly, nourished by their only source of food, which are the plants leaves and stems. It takes about four weeks for the monarch to fully emerge. They then follow a sleep and feeding pattern governed by a circadian clock in their brain, an organ no bigger than the head of a pin. I find that extremely interesting, don't you Mr. Harmon"?

"Very much so Josie. I can guess that you, Monica and Emily have a lot in common to discuss". Looking at the audience, he said "Did that sound like a conversation between a five year old and a couple of twelve years old?

These children are so advanced in their intellectual capacity, it's beyond my understanding. Tell me something Josie, what do you think of the twins' ability to communicate with animals?"

"I think it's grand, really cool!" she replied.

After this bit of conversation, he asked Josie how she planned to impress the members of the audience, to which she replied "We should never try to impress other people Mr. Harmon, but we should always act in a way that comes to us naturally".

"How right you are Josie. Thank you for reminding me. Tell us then, what comes to you naturally"?

"Music is what comes naturally to me, so I will play my violin and also the piano which I've learned to play in the past three months, since our last visit to Saint John. My Mom and Dad suggested that we bring my keyboard because it was easy to bring. Shall I begin"?

"Is it going to be the piece you already played for me and Danelle ?"

"Yes, Mr. Harmon, that would be it".

"Ladies and gentlemen, the keyboard will fail to give this little girl justice, but here is Josie Quinlan to play one of Mozart's favourite compositions. Enjoy"!

And enjoy they did! The sound of the little keyboard resonated throughout the Imperial Theatre. When she was done, the fans stood up and clapped and cheered and indicated they wanted more. Once the audience seated themselves again, she played one more piece on her keyboard and then, one piece on the violin, after which she bowed and waved to everyone and looked toward Danelle who had become very emotional listening to this little girl. Moments later she and Joel walked back on stage to join Josie.

"Josie, there are no words to express the emotion I felt during your performance. It was purely and truly inspiring, so please; don't ever give up your gift of music," Danelle told her.

Addressing the audience, Joel said "I honestly believe

we were visited by a wingless cherub tonight. What a great performance! Thank you so much Josie for closing our last show with such beautiful music. And our heartfelt thanks to your Mom and Dad for bringing you all the way from Stratford, Ontario. Danelle and I will be forever grateful that you made tonight such a memorable evening, for us as well as for everyone here. Tom will now accompany you backstage honey, where you can chat some more with Monica and Emily".

"Thank you Mr and Mrs. Harmon for inviting me, and I think Arielle is the cutest baby in the whole world!"

*****

It was time to say goodbye one last time.

"As I've stressed many times during these past years, 'for everything there is a season'. Therefore my dear people, the time has come to move on. Thank you for the continued support you have showed Danelle and I throughout my 'first' career. I will keep these special memories of you, the fans who made our show possible, and for all the guests who made the show interesting. I have learned so much from everyone who shared their special gifts and talents with us".

"I give all credit to the One True God for allowing me to develop my abilities and especially for bringing Danelle and Arielle into my life. He works in such mysterious ways"!

"Like a good parent, He watches over us always and His legacy to humankind is that one day, we will be set free from our physical restrictions, that is as soon as our 'time out' has proved to be effective. Until then, may the God of our ancestors continue to protect us from harm, guide us and lead us through His only begotten Son, our Lord Jesus Christ, who is the Way, the Truth and the Life".

The curtains closed and hand in hand, Joel and Danelle, with baby Arielle in her arms, turned and walked backstage one last time.

Epilogue

Joel Harmon believed that religion was a personal choice, not to be forced upon anyone. Only by examples could he point the way to eternal life. He had had a glimpse of that life and so did Danelle. They knew for certain that God was real and they could only testify to the fact that although life ends, it also continues on in a different way, in a different dimension. Doesn't the lowly caterpillar leave his cocoon behind to become a beautiful butterfly? So will we, because we are all 'drawn to the light'!

Amen to that!